I'D RATHER GO OUT SMILING

DONN WEINHOLTZ

I'd Rather Go Out Smiling

All Rights Reserved © 2024 by Donn Weinholtz

No part of this book may be reproduced or transmitted in any form or by any means, graphic, electronic, or mechanical, including photocopying, recording, taping, or by any information storage retrieval system, without the written permission of the publisher.

CONTENTS

Dedication	v
Acknowledgements	vii
Foreword	ix
Why Write About It?	xiii
1. Home for Christmas	1
2. Depression and War	19
3. Good Years	36
4. Missing	62
5. Oat Cell	77
6. At Both Ends	102
7. "The Great Storm is Over"	126
8. I'd Rather Go Out Smiling	144
9. Final Journey	165
10. Aftershocks	189
11. Reflections	205
12. And Then...	209
About the Author	237

DEDICATION

To Our Family

ACKNOWLEDGEMENTS

Many people contributed to this book's two editions. My immediate and extended families remained encouraging throughout, never complaining about me embarrassing them. Rob Fried, Joe Olzacki, Ted Sizer, Bill Taylor and my wife, Diane, provided extensive comments on various drafts. George Brophy and Karen Will assisted with invaluable copy editing. Kerry Mickle, at iUniverse, guided me through the initial publication process, and our son, Phil, at Full Media Services, oversaw the second.

Phil also attentively curated the books's photo and document collection, while also providing valuable insights based on his personal, family research. His loving attention to accuracy, detail, and efficiency continually amaze me.

Many Quaker "Friends" at Hartford Monthly Meeting were highly supportive. And Joe Mullan lined up one of the earliest reviews and offered to peddle copies of the first edition on the Ocean City boardwalk.

Thanks to all.

FOREWORD

In 2002, I published an earlier version of this book entitled, *Longing to Live... Learning to Die.* It was well received by many who read it, including some highly qualified reviewers. For example, Stephanie Weinrich, the former director of the United Kingdom's Natural Death Center, commented: *I would highly recommend Longing to Live... Learning to Die to anyone who has ever sat by the deathbed of a friend or relative, anyone who has ever wondered how they would cope with their parents' death, anyone who works in the field or who has interest in patient welfare.* And psychiatrist William Taylor wrote: *Donn Weinholtz had me crying and laughing, more times than I can remember, with his deeply felt family story of love, hope, humor, frustration, acceptance of illness and struggles with death. If I could use only one book to teach young therapists how resiliency sustains a healthy family, I'd choose this one."*

    I'm issuing an updated edition so a new generation of readers might benefit from this book. The intervening twenty-plus years have brought new experiences, and taught new lessons, about the loss of family members and close friends. In particular, my wife, Diane, and I have served most of this period on the Memorial Committee of Hartford Friends (Quaker) Meeting. In this capacity, we have met with many grieving people, while helping them plan the celebrations of their loved ones' lives. And I have frequently officiated at these simultaneously solemn and joyful occasions. For Diane and me, being able to provide comfort to others during their difficult transitions has been extraordinarily meaningful. While these events are not chronicled here, they have deeply influenced my perceptions of our own family's experiences.

Another factor affecting my decision to issue a revised edition is that I'm now an elderly guy, a senior citizen, an old man. I have a much richer appreciation of what it's like for my own body to be falling apart. I occasionally, wonder how many years I have left. Things look and feel different on the other side of seventy. They are different.

Finally, when I finished writing *Longing to Live...Learning to Die*, I was emotionally drained and couldn't handle writing anything more about death and dying. I needed a break. Consequently, my next book, *Carolina Blue*, was a complete reversal; a comic mystery/adventure novella intended to be a fun, easy read, not at all emotionally taxing. It was followed by many other writing and editing projects, not remotely related to death. Now, having had years to recover, I'm again ready to address the task.

Regarding the book's new title, I almost chose *I'd Rather Go Out Smiling* the first time around, but decided to use it as a chapter title instead because I wanted there to be no doubt that this was a death and dying book. Then, over the years, a few readers suggested *I'd Rather Go Out Smiling* as the book title. Now, it feels right that it graces the cover. My Mom, Agathe (Gada) Weinholtz, is the core inspirational figure of the book. They were her words, and they capture her spirit.

If you previously read *Longing to Live... Learning to Die*, and you have a fantastic memory, you'll notice that twelve chapters of *I'd Rather Go Out Smiling* vary little from the original book. This forward, a set of photographs that I was previously unable to include, and the concluding chapter, are the new materials. The final chapter, *And Then...*, doesn't contain the in-depth descriptions and detailed dialogues included before it. That's because I didn't take notes immediately following the events described, as I never expected to be writing about them. So, when materials appear as quotations, please recognize that they are my best efforts at reconstructing unrecorded discussions.

WHY WRITE ABOUT IT?

This book focuses primarily on several deaths that shook my family during the 1990's. While I was writing it, I told my niece, Lynn, at a family gathering about the outline for the book, which had only recently crystallized for me. My older cousin, Donna, overheard the conversation and asked,

"Why? Why do you want to write about all of that? For catharsis? To write a best seller? Why?"

They were good questions, which deserve a more thorough response than I was able to give at the time.

Certainly, I had a strong need for catharsis. While it's not unusual to have close relatives die, having several pass away in rapid succession, under especially trying circumstances, takes its toll. Writing was a good, productive way of coping. Also, when you love people very much you realize that their funeral services and obituaries simply don't do justice to them. I wanted to record these stories to share the richness of my family members' lives. Following each death, I learned how comforting the condolences from others who have suffered similar losses can be. There is great relief in knowing that you are not alone; that, in fact, you are just one of the vast number of people recovering from the deaths of loved ones. However, while others will often open up to you in conversations about dealing with death, few write about such experiences in any detail. I'm convinced that it is important to expand the easily accessible literature on encounters with dying. I also believe this should be done with gentle humor, as laughing and smiling are so important to healing.

Regarding Donna's question about trying to write a best seller, I know the odds of the publication game and have few illusions. In fact, I can imagine my mother saying:

"Donn, if you want to try to make a few bucks by writing this book, go ahead and do it. God knows, you're going to be paying through the nose with three kids in college. You might as well get what you can. But do you really think anybody is going to want to read about us?"

I guess we will see. It is so hard to break through the massive oceans of information that accumulate, daily, in the modern world. Can people even find the book to read a few pages and see if they want to continue? I wonder about this, continually. Then I'll get an email, out-of-the-blue, such as that from a nurse practitioner thanking me for writing *Longing to Live...Learning to Die*, which she found in a used bookstore. She was deeply moved and wished other nurses could read it. Ah, hope springs eternal. Maybe this time around?

Some of the dialogue in the book is practically verbatim, based on notes that I took soon after events occurred. Other conversations, however, are paraphrased from memory. With the exception of family friends, Dr. Benjamin Bell and Ms. Ethel Biddle, I have altered the names of all health professionals.

1

HOME FOR CHRISTMAS

"Please, Dad! Do it for me."
"No."
"Come on. How about it?"
"No!"

I had hoped to gently persuade my elderly father into flying fromFlorida to Philadelphia, but he insisted on driving. Growing desperate, I began drawing on every argument that I could muster.

"Dad, Mom told me that she didn't want you to drive it again. She swore the two of you would fly this year."

"No."

"But, Dad, you got lost last year!"

The previous December, during their ritual trek home for Christmas, Mom and Dad had taken the Auto Train from Florida to Lorton, Virginia. Then they drove from Lorton to Philadelphia, but wandered around Philly for hours before eventually finding my brother's house in the northern suburbs. At the time, they were both seventy-nine, and Dad remained mildly disoriented following a stroke that he had suffered three years earlier. Mom, who died the following May, was still sharp as a tack; but her health was frail. Afterward, she was certain that they couldn't handle another driving fiasco.

"You know, Donn, I had to drive the whole way from Virginia to Bill's house. Your father kept telling me how tired he was and how he couldn't see right, and I didn't know where in the hell we were. I was exhausted by the time we got there. It was all I could do to crawl into bed. I don't care what your father says. Next year we are flying."

Dad - William F Weinholtz

Unfortunately, invoking Mom's argument had no impact either.

"No."

"What if you get sick?"

"I'll pull over and stay in a motel until I get better."

"How are you going to handle the Washington Beltway?"

"I'll drive fifty miles per hour in the right lane. I know it like the back of my hand."

"Dad, you got lost in a mall at Christmas last year. The year before", when they did fly due to Mom's summer quadruple bypass surgery, "you got lost in the airport. Ten years ago, when you were coming to visit us in Iowa, you took a wrong turn in St. Louis, and drove two hundred miles out of your away across Missouri."

"No!"

I realized that the situation was only deteriorating; but, hoping for a miracle, I continued.

"What if it snows?

"I'll find a motel! Donn, I don't want to talk about this any longer."

"Dad, you might have an accident. You not only could hurt yourself, you could hurt or kill others, maybe a family with small kids."

"No. I won't do that. I'll know when to stop driving. I'll know when it gets dangerous. Damn it! I want my car."

"Why is it so important, Dad?"

"Well, I have to take Betty and Milt", Dad's sister and her husband, "out to lunch."

Aunt Betty, sometime during the 1940's

"Dad! They live right around the corner from Bill. He can loan you a car to do that."

"No. I like my car, and I want it in case I have to run out to the store for something."

Totally exasperated. I fell silent. "Donn, are you still there?"

"Yeah, Dad, but I am terribly disappointed. I'm only arguing with you because I love you. I wouldn't be worried if I knew that you could still do things like get out and hit a golf ball, but you can't. Dad, even though you might think you are your same old self, you aren't. Please don't do it."

"Donn, let's stop this now. I'm driving up, or I am going to take the Auto Train, and that is final!"

At last a concession! He might take the Auto Train. That would still leave the worst part of the drive, but I could go down to Washington, from our home in Connecticut, and pick him up.

"Okay, Dad, you win. But if you take the Auto Train, please let me or Bill, come down to meet you and drive you to Philadelphia."

"No. I am going to do it myself. I've got to go now. The Dolphins game is coming on, and we've talked enough. Goodbye, Donn."

"Bye, Dad."

I felt awful. I had never unloaded like that on Dad before, and I surely hadn't wanted to do it to him just four months after Mom had died. Still, I felt like I had no choice; the potential for an accident was so high, and I was the only person likely to seriously confront him. Fortunately, he had backed down a little. Maybe if Bill followed up…

Bill and Donn

Bill and I have always been brothers; even though, technically, we are "half " brothers. Bill's biological father was also named Bill, Bill Smith. The last name differentiated him from Dad, Bill Weinholtz. Mom, whose name was Agathe, but who was known to all by the Danish nickname, Gada, used to joke that she planned it that way.

"I made sure that when I remarried I wouldn't get myself into trouble by confusing their names. Even if I accidentally meant Bill Smith when I was calling 'Bill', your father wouldn't know the difference."

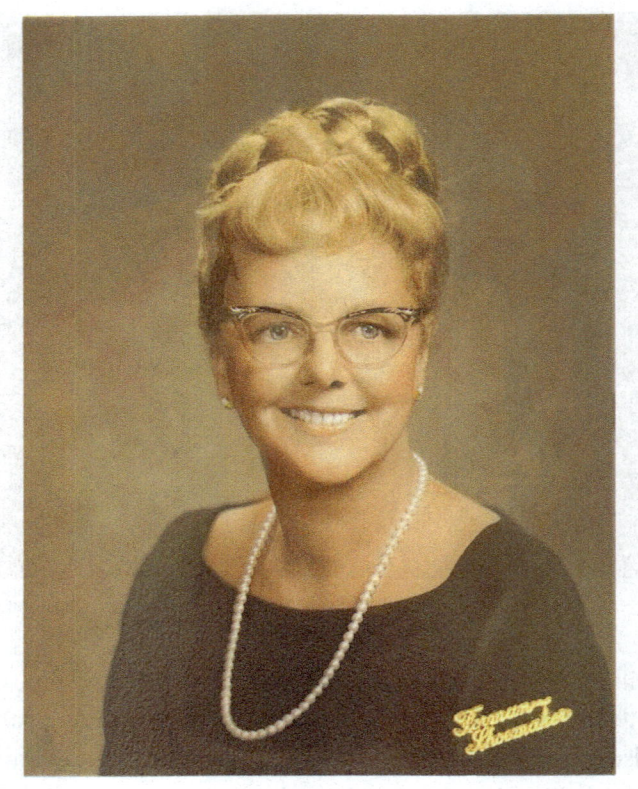

Mom, circa 1965

Bill Smith died at thirty-three from heart failure associated with child-hood rheumatic fever. Dad adopted my brother, Bill, and our sister, Nancy, soon after Mom and Dad's wedding on September 2, 1948, when Bill was nine and Nancy was eleven. I came along on October 1, 1949. Mom had dated Dad in high school, but she dropped him to marry Bill Smith. As Mom told it:

"Bill Smith was extremely good looking, and he could play the piano very well. He played by ear, and he could sit down and play almost anything immediately after he heard it for the first time. He was real persuasive too. I was still awfully young, and he just kept talking and talking. The next thing I knew he had convinced me that I ought to marry him."

Mom was just seventeen at the time, and Bill Smith's proposal was probably aided by the fact that she was upset with my grandmother and Mom's stepfather for forbidding her from going to nursing school.

"I was so angry that they weren't going to let me do what I had always wanted to do. I figured that I would show them a thing or two."

So, she and Bill Smith were married in 1931, but they decided to keep it a secret until Mom was eighteen and finished with high school. Then, for some reason, unknown to me, Mom had second thoughts about her marriage. After graduating, instead of joining Bill Smith, she went off to Denmark, where my grandparents had been born and where Mom had spent much of her first seven years, to visit relatives. After five or six months, she returned to the U.S.; but still keeping the marriage a secret, she moved back in with her mother and stepfather. However, it didn't take long before there was another disagreement, during which Mom announced that she was already married and that she was moving in with her husband.

Not surprisingly, this erratic start was followed by a rocky marriage. I'm not sure about all of the problems, but I do know that Bill Smith had a bad temper. Mom once told me that, initially, she could deal with it, but she started giving up on the relationship when she saw the effect that his outbursts were having on Nancy and Bill.

"He would go into a rage and the two of them would come and hide behind me. They would be crying and and shivering with fear. I started thinking, 'This is crazy, enough is enough!'"

So, Mom packed up the kids and left him. She even began dating Dad again. But her conscience got the best of her, and she moved back.

"I knew that his health was bad, and that he didn't have long to live. I just couldn't let him die alone without his children."

When Bill Smith eventually died, Mom and Dad didn't waste any time getting back together. Dad's official line was:

"I saw his obituary in the newspaper. I waited an appropriate amount of time, then I asked your mother to go out."

But as Mom told it:

"Oh, your father was just telling you that to make things look proper. The fact is that Bill Smith was only in the ground for a few weeks when I called your father up and asked him over for dinner."

The Weinholtz Family (Mom, Bill, Nancy, Donn and Dad)

They were married within a year, and remained happily so until Mom's death in 1994. Along the way, they withstood their fair share of challenges, including brother Bill's adolescence.

Young Bill

Though bright, Bill hated school and persistently blew off homework in favor of working part-time at a local Mobil station. He even purposely flunked an entire year of school so he had to go to summer school; thereby avoiding spending his vacation at our summer home in Ocean City, New Jersey. Bill couldn't have cared less about the beach. So, he stayed at home with Dad during the week, only coming down to the shore on weekends. After morning summer school classes, while Dad was at work, Bill pumped gas at a local Mobil station and worked on cars, all afternoon.

The most dramatic of Bill's escapades, that I can remember, involved running away to Florida with a few of his friends. To his credit, he sent postcards and called home to keep us alerted about his safety. Still, the incident was particularly hard on Mom and Dad; especially since, at the time, Dad was serving as chair of our local school board.

Marine Bill

Later, Bill dropped out of school; did a two-year hitch in the Marines; returned to school; dropped out again; and obtained his Graduate Equivalency Degree. Always a hard worker at whatever he enjoyed, he found good, stable office work, but stumbled into an unfortunate marriage by getting his girlfriend pregnant. Despite immediate relationship problems, Bill and his first wife, Penny, had five children in rapid succession, before divorcing. After the break-up, Bill retained custody of the five boys. Then, he got married, happily, to Edie, who had three children of her own. Somehow, even with eight kids, they persisted. Despite the shaky early years, as time went by, Dad and Bill grew much closer. After weathering the struggles of child-rearing, Bill became particularly appreciative of all that Dad had done for him, and Dad returned the affection. The two of them enjoyed golfing followed by smoking, drinking, and having lunch at whatever course they happened to be playing. While I liked the golfing and eating, when we were all together, I usually chose not to drink and regularly harassed them both for smoking cigarettes. Also, as an adult, I became a pacifist and a Democrat, traits that irked Dad and didn't tarnish Bill. During all those years, while growing up, I was the fair-haired boy who could do no wrong, but later in the ball game Bill kept looking better and better to our World War II veteran and Republican Dad.

Bill and Edie's Sons - K.C., Ray, Terry, Billy and David (absent Randy & Kris)

So, it was plausible that Bill might have more leverage than me in trying to get Dad to show some common sense. I gave him a call.

"Well, Bill, I gave it my best shot; but I didn't get too far. The most that I could get him to concede was that he 'might' take the Auto Train; but even if he does, he wants to drive up to Philly from D.C. on his own."

"He's a stubborn old bird."

"I'll say! Still, there might be hope. I was really hard on him. Maybe you can call him, take the high road, and convince him to let you pick him up outside of Washington. Feel free to make me out as the bad guy. You never know, it just might work."

Bill and Edie's Daughter, Nina.

"Okay," Bill chuckled. "I'll give him a call. I've got to talk to him anyway about Edie and me coming down for Thanksgiving. I'll just happen to slip in the idea about picking him up at Christmas. But you know, if he's really pissed off, I'll have to change the topic."

"Yeah, I know. Thanks, Bill. And, again, feel free to stick it to me if you think that will help. Tell him how I haven't been the same since Mom died, and that I am worrying too much. Tell him that I told you how it is interfering with my work. Tell him anything that you can think of."

"Alright. I'll give it a try, and I'll get back in touch with you in a few days."

I didn't have to wait long. Bill called the next night. "Well, how did it go?" I asked hopefully.

"To be honest with you, Donn, I never even got a chance to ask him. As soon as I finished with the arrangements for our trip down at Thanksgiving, he ripped into you and wouldn't let me get a word in. He went on and on about the fact that you call too often and won't let him have any peace."

That one really hurt. I had been calling maybe five times a

week since Mom died, but for the most part they had been seemed like really good conversations. Usually, Dad didn't want to hang up, chatting on long after I had expected us to finish.

"Jesus!" I thought to myself, "I must have really put him on the warpath. He's never been that mad at me."

Well, there was the time he blew up when he walked in the front door of our house in Ocean City and saw my "McCarthy for President" poster hanging where anybody who entered the house could see it; but that was an exception. In general, Dad had always found ways to rationalize away the problems he had with me. In the case of my pacifism, he once came up with:

"Donn, you just aren't the type. You're not capable of going off to war. If they draft you, I'm volunteering to go in your place."

Dad, WWII

Fortunately, Dad, who was in his late sixties at the time, never had to show up in uniform at his local recruitment center ready to deliver on his pledge.

Even though I was taken aback by Bill's report on the intensity of Dad's response, I kept calling Dad, knowing that the problem would soon blow over. He had indicated to Bill that he definitely was going to take the Auto Train, and I tried several times over the next few weeks to get Dad to agree to me picking him up in Virginia; but the answer was always the same, and his tone was always slightly irritated. So, I was incredibly relieved when Bill called and laid out "the plan."

"You're going to love this. We're sending Billy", Bill's 34 year old son, "down to D.C. on the train. He'll meet Dad and drive him up to our place."

"Great, are you going to tell Dad?"

"Hell, no! That would kill everything. It will be a big surprise.-Billy will tell him that he was vacationing in Washington, and since he just happened to be down there, he thought it would be nice if they could drive up together. Even If Dad catches on, what's he going to do! He can't leave Billy standing there."

It was perfect! Highly manipulative, but the ends clearly justified the means.

"Bill, Mom would be proud of you. You're obviously her son."

"Yeah, the apple doesn't fall far from the tree. Maybe the old girl was up there sending me the idea."

The evening of the day that Billy delivered Dad to Bill and Edie's, I called to welcome him, and to see how the trip had gone. Still sensitive to his anger over our previous discussions about the journey home, I was clueless as to how he was going to react to having been picked up. It didn't take long for me to find out.

"Boy, was I happy to see Billy! I wasn't able to sleep at all on that damned train, with all that clackety-clacking. If Billy hadn't been there, I couldn't have made it."

I wanted to say, "I told you so." And I wanted to follow it up with, "This is proof that you need to fly the next time." But, I bit my tongue. I was so relieved to know that Dad had arrived safely, and I wasn't going to ruin things by getting into a petty argument. It was good to have him stowed away in a safe place for the holidays. Of course, as soon as I had registered those thoughts, he followed up with:

"That does it for me. Next year I am going to drive the whole way by myself."

A few days later, I decided to press my luck and invite Dad to spend the week with us in Connecticut. My family includes my wife, Diane, and our children: David, who was fourteen at the time; Philip; who was ten; and Jenny, who was six. I was pretty sure that I knew the answer before I asked, but I floated the idea anyway.

"Dad, we'd all love to see you, and it will give Edie and Bill a break from having company. We could even bring your car up here so you'll have it to get around. What do you say?"

"Donn, don't pressure me. I'll see you all down here on Christmas Eve. Then you and David will be flying down to Florida in February for my birthday. Now that I am up here, I just want to sit."

I was disappointed, but it would have been a great surprise if Dad had agreed. He had always been set in his ways, and at eighty he was even more a creature of habit. At Bill's, he had his favorite chair strategically placed across from the TV in the den. It came with a floor lamp that allowed him to do the New York Times Crossword Puzzle during the day and to read action novels late into the night. He could smoke his Winstons inside, and there weren't any young kids around to engage him in unnecessary conversation. He knew where the liquor cabinet was, and Betty and Milt lived only five minutes away. Why spoil all of this by traipsing off to Connecticut!

Dad and his "Cough Syrup"

As things turned out, it was a wise decision on his part. Dad managed to have a good time, even though it was his first Christmas without Mom. He took the entire extended family, about thirty of us, out for Christmas Eve dinner. He watched every conceivable holiday football game. He treated Betty and Milt to lunch; and he regularly insisted on taking Edie and Bill to supper at his old haunts, in particular the Springhouse Tavern, where he still knew some of the waitresses. He smoked and he drank. He was so relaxed that he even shocked Edie and Bill one evening by agreeing to visit their son David, his wife, Sabrina, and their two young daughters. While there, he hoisted the girls into his lap and he belted out Christmas carols in his still surprisingly strong, tenor voice.

During those few weeks that Dad was in Philadelphia, Bill provided me with regular updates on how things were going. As I heard how Dad was enjoying himself, I surmised that his stroke had turned out to be something of a blessing. Although he sometimes was a bit detached from everyone around him, he wasn't wallowing in the despair that we all feared would engulf him following Mom's death. His calm was all the more remarkable because prior to the stroke he was easily brought to sobs at the thought of losing her. Because his speech merely displayed the occasional lapses you might expect of someone his age, and his memory was generally quite good; it seemed to me that the primary after-effect of the stroke was an attention span ever-so-slightly short-circuited in a way that prevented him from spiraling downward into depression.

Just five weeks after Mom's funeral when Diane, Phil, Jenny and I dropped David off at a camp in Tennessee and drove on to visit Dad at his condominium in Stuart, Florida; Dad had some melancholy moments, but he always managed to quickly shake them. After tearing up for a minute or two, he'd pick up his crossword puzzle or one of his novels, and soon appear to be fine. If not turning to those outlets, he'd start watching baseball, "Wheel of Fortune," or David Letterman, who he talked about as though he was a personal friend, while repeatedly saying, "I can't stand that Jay Leno." By the time that Phil and I flew down for a long weekend around my birthday in October, it was clear that Dad had also forged a social life for himself around his almost nightly trips to his two favorite restaurants, The Olive Garden—one left turn and a few miles north on U.S. 1—and Gentleman Jim's—one right turn and a few miles south on U.S. 1. He was well known at both places. The waitresses doted on him, and he handed out very healthy tips.

Mom had predicted as much.

"Donn, if I go first, Dad is going to be fine. Just you wait and see. He won't have to worry about upkeep here." (Their condo had three rooms, a sun porch and a small kitchenette.) "He knows his way to the stores and to the doctor's. He'll go to Gentleman Jim's and The Olive Garden five or six times a week; and Aunt Ruth", Mom's wonderfully fit girlhood friend, and my godmother, who lived in the next building, "will look in on him. Believe me, everything will be okay."

Although experience had taught me never to question the

accuracy of Mom's predictions, I was still surprised and impressed by Dad's resilience. I surely didn't want him out on the road driving long distances, but I was awed by how well he was holding together. The more that I thought about it, the more I realized that he always had been a survivor. In contrast to my own life, which had been remarkably smooth, even sheltered, Dad's first forty years had involved potentially life-shattering challenges that I could barely imagine. I felt small for having underestimated him.

2

DEPRESSION AND WAR

Born in Philadelphia on February 6, 1914, Dad was the youngest of William ("Will") Frederick Weinholtz's and Carolina ("Carrie") Wilhemina Eckhardt Weinholtz's six children. Dad's brother, Russell, died at less than a year, six years before Dad was born. His sister, Kathryn, died at six before Dad turned two. His other siblings Helen, Harold and Betty all lived long lives and were much a part of my childhood and young adult life. My paternal grandparents, however, remain mysteries to me, as both died before I was born. I do know that Will and Carrie were the children of German immigrants who settled in the Kensington section of Philadelphia. The city was distinctly segregated by ethnicity and religion, and the Weinholtz and Eckhardt families participated in their German Baptist Church, where Will and Carrie may have met. Carrie was a skilled pianist; and after her marriage to Will, taught students from their home.Will ventured into carpet sales, traveling a fair amount with frequent overnight trips.

When I was growing up, Dad occasionally referred to my grandmother as "the best friend" that he ever had. When Mom surprised him one Christmas with a retouched photo of my grandmother, he sat motionless, for what seemed like an eternity, staring at the picture through tear-filled eyes.

Grandmother "Carrie" Weinholtz

On the other hand, Dad's references to my grandfather were few, far-between and rarely favorable.

"My father was the smartest person I ever knew, but he always thought of himself before anybody else. Your grandmother sacrificed so many things for all of us, but not my father. He always came first."

Grandfather "Will Weinholtz, 1927

"I wanted to join the Boy Scouts more than anything else in the world, but he claimed that they were too militaristic, and he wouldn't let me. Harold..." (who was ten years older) "...was allowed to join., but not me. I cried and I cried, but he wouldn't budge."

"Nobody in our family loved my father any more than me, and nobody cried any harder than me when he died. Still, I'll never be able to forgive him for what he did to us, and I'll never do anything like that to your mother and you."

This last comment came out of left field one evening when I was about fifteen, while Dad and I were driving through Philadelphia on our way to the shore. I wouldn't have had the vaguest idea what he was talking about if not for the fact that a year or so before I happened to ask Mom how my Grandfather Weinholtz had died.

"You mean you don't know. Your father never told you!"

"No. He's never said a word about it. So, how'd he die?"

"He committed suicide."

I was stunned, and didn't want to believe what I'd just heard. Though it wasn't at all like Mom to do so, I convinced myself that she was playing a cruel joke.

"Come on, Mom. Don't kid around about something like that. Tell me the truth."

"I am, Donn. He committed suicide."

"Oh my God. How'd he...how'd he do it?"

"He hung himself. It was during the Depression. Dad came home one day and found your grandfather hanging there. I'm sorry. I thought you knew."

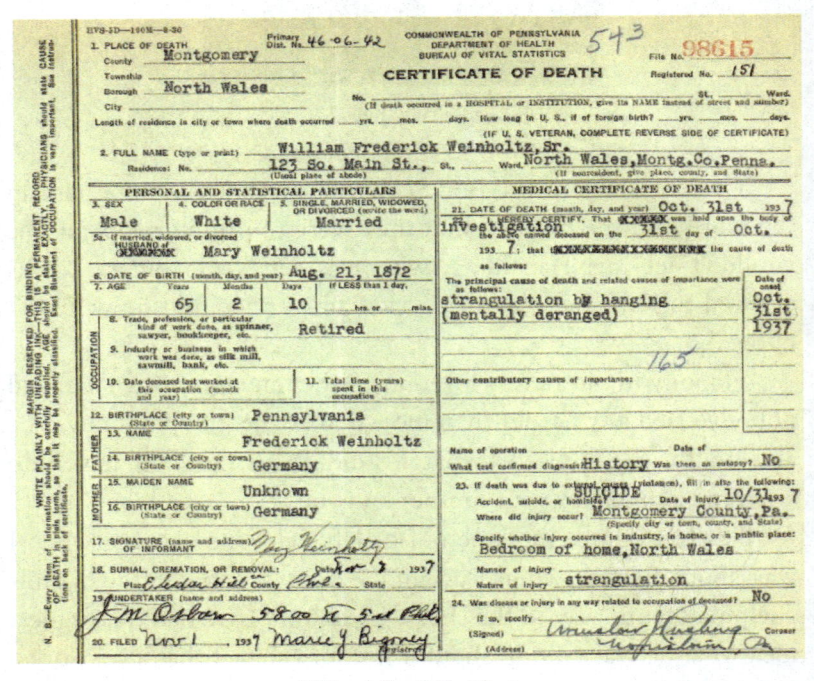

William's Death Certificate

"Nobody ever told me anything. Jesus, no wonder Dad doesn't talk about him. What happened? Why'd he do it?"

"I'm not sure. He must have been badly depressed. His business was failing. Those were hard times. A lot of people couldn't handle it. Your grandfather wasn't alone. There were a lot of suicides."

Even if he was in good company, the thought of being the direct descendent of a suicide victim didn't sit well. Though haunted by the usual adolescent insecurities, I took comfort in the fact that I was a well-adjusted guy supported by a nurturing, equally well-adjusted family. But in a single moment that whole picture was challenged. My head was spinning with questions. Were there other skeletons in the family closet? What must it have been like for Dad, and how had it affected him all of these years? Was knowing going to affect me? Is mental illness hereditary?

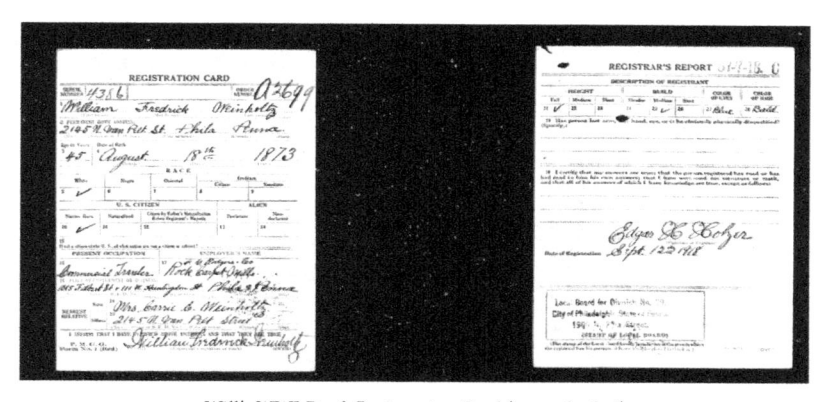

Will's WWI Draft Registration Card (never drafted)

Prior to Mom's disclosure, my most vivid association when I thought of "The Depression" was of "spinach sandwiches." As a kid, whenever I was fussing over my dinner, Dad used to get worked up and tell me some variation of:

"You don't know how good you have it, Donn. During The Depression, things were so bad that all we could afford was spinach sandwiches. It broke my mother's heart not to be able to give us more, but she couldn't; and we didn't complain. So, I don't want to hear anything else out of you, young man. You're not leaving this table until you've finished everything on that plate." Even now, when my mind turns to The Depression, I still think of spinach sandwiches. But I also imagine my frantic father cutting the rope and lowering his father's body to the ground. Over time, awareness of my grandfather's suicide heightened my respect for Dad. I eventually realized that, while he was weathering losing Mom to Bill Smith, he also suffered the worst kind of tragedy; yet he came through his traumas remaining deeply devoted to those he loved. I had always sensed that Dad was somebody who committed for the long haul, but for years I hadn't realized just how thoroughly the rules he lived by were seared into his soul. The extent of Dad's steadfastness, however, was never lost on Mom. In spite of her occasional grumbling about some of Dad's stubborn, even antisocial, behaviors; she remained deeply touched that he had taken her back with two kids and with my grandmother, who lived with them for nearly thirty years.

Donn, Nancy and Bill, 1957

"Your father is a good man, Donn. There are very few people who would have done what he did. He always treated Nancy and

Bill as though they were his own, and he never complained once about your grandmother. That really says something."

In the years immediately following my grandfather's death, Dad went on to complete a bachelor's degree in mechanical engineering, and he subsequently also managed to pickup master's degrees in math and physics. The Depression made engineering jobs hard to find, and Dad wandered into school teaching as a fallback profession. He taught math and shop within the Philadelphia school system; and while teaching may not have been his first love, the vacation schedule allowed him to pursue his wide-ranging interests. He sang in churches around the city. He dabbled in oil painting, and made some money on the side as a commercial artist. He pitched a little semi-pro baseball, and even raced midget race cars, once telling me:

"I used to race under the name of Billy Wood because between the wars there was so much anti-German sentiment that I didn't dare use my real name. If they had announced 'Weinholtz', someone in the stands might have thrown oil on the track in front of my car to make me crash."

While teaching, Dad continued to live with my grandmother, whose health was poor. He must have been a great help around the house, as he was thoroughly devoted to her; and Dad was a pretty fair carpenter who could also lay brick, fix most electrical problems, tile floors and do plumbing. He loved that kind of handiwork, and later in life often had some sort of home renovation project underway.

Dad's WWII Draft Card

When Dad finally left my grandmother's home, it wasn't for happy reasons. Rather than waiting to be drafted, he enlisted to fight in World War II. War was indeed "Hell" for Dad, exacting a terrible psychic toll; but I never once heard him question whether or not what he had done was right. He lived out his life in the certainty that Hitler had to be defeated. Clear about this responsibility, Dad joined the Army immediately after Pearl Harbor. He rose to the rank of sergeant in the Tank Corps, and fought in fierce combat in North Africa and Europe; participating in the Battle of the Bulge and the conquest of Germany. He twice told me about being found unconscious in a foxhole next to the body of a dead German soldier, who Dad had apparently shot at close range. It may have been during that episode that Dad had his teeth knocked out. It was a guarded secret that Dad wore dentures. I never knew it until ninth grade when I got braces. Suddenly very tooth conscious, I commented to Mom how impressed I was with Dad's almost perfect teeth. Laughing heartily, she again let the cat out of the bag.

"Of course they're straight. They're not his! He lost them all in The War."

Dad's disclosures of his war experiences were about as infrequent as his comments on the merits of Polident. Other than the "dead German in the foxhole" story, I can only recall ever hearing a few other comments.

"I went in the Army at 180 pounds, and I came out at 115. I was nothing more than a skeleton."

William F Weinholtz, WWII

"I participated in the shelling of our family's ancestral town. I hated to do it, but it had to be done. It's horrible to say, but the Germans, even if we were related to them, got what they deserved."

"I'm sorry, Donn, but you'll never get me to go camping with you. I spent the better part of three years sleeping on the ground in a pup tent in all kinds of weather, and I can't stand the thought of ever sleeping in any kind of tent again."

"Before The War, I used to love to hunt, and I had four or five rifles in the house. Afterwards, I sold them all. I never wanted to see another gun in my life."

Dad's WWII Honorable Discharge

Most memorably, when I was a young boy Dad passionately told me:

"I don't ever want to see you point a gun at anyone! That goes for any kind of gun, even a toy gun. You can never be sure that it's not real and that it won't hurt someone."

And when I protested, he responded:

"Donn, you're only five years old, and don't know anything about guns. I know all about how dangerous they are. I was in The War."

So, I took this message very seriously, and for years I was the only kid in my neighborhood who had toy guns, but refused to point them at anyone. Furthermore, I preached to my friends that they shouldn't be pointing their guns at anyone either. When I told them what my father, who was "in The War," had said; they told me I was crazy because toy guns couldn't hurt anybody. And I told them that they didn't know what they were talking about because their fathers hadn't been "in The War."

Ironically, the fact that I so thoroughly absorbed Dad's intense revulsion towards guns eventually caused a conflict between us. While at Dickinson College in Carlisle, Pennsylvania, I lasted only one year in Army R.O.T.C. I disliked calling people, "Sir." I saw no sense in polishing my brass buttons and spit shining my shoes. And while marching in formation, I refused to chant: "I'm in the Army hear my song. I'm gonna shoot a VietCong." But the final straw came when we went out to a firing range, and I had to shoot my rifle at a human-shaped target. I was horrified as my bullets shredded the cardboard figure.

I silently screamed to myself, "My, God! They really want me to kill people. Screw them. I'm quitting."

And I did. I waited until the end of the semester, and I didn't call home to tell my folks until it was a done deal. This was well before Dad had decided that he was going to volunteer in my place in case I was drafted, and he didn't take the news too well. It was 1968, and the Vietnam War was escalating. Dad argued that if I did have to go, I would be far better off as an officer than as a draftee. I don't think he expected what he got back.

"Dad, I don't care. I'm not going. You told me never to point a gun at someone, and I can't do it. I mean what the hell ever happened to 'Thou shalt not kill?' The commandment isn't, 'Thou shalt not kill, except under certain circumstances.'"

"Donn, this is your country. It's war. We've got to stand up to the Communists, or they'll walk all over us…", and then throwing me a curve, he loudly added "…I did what I did because I had to. I didn't want to, but I had to!"

There was an awkward pause during which I sensed that we had entered a zone, in Dad's own life, that neither of us knew how to negotiate. So, I looked for a way to get off of the phone.

"Yeah, I know, Dad. Let's talk about this later. I don't know what I'll do, but I've got three more years of college deferment. The war will probably be over by then anyway. I'll talk to you next week."

Of course, the war didn't end according to my timetable; and my military fate loomed larger with each passing semester. Then, during my junior year, the Nixon administration, under the pressure of increasing war protests and uneven draft board performances, instituted the draft lottery. At colleges across the nation, the official lottery drawing, conducted in Washington D.C. using a rotating basket full of ping pong balls, became the biggest event of the year.

By then I was a college junior and a resident advisor in one of the freshman dorms. The guys on my floor decided to get a keg to celebrate, or drown our sorrows, as our numbers were read in descending order of doom from the AP wire by one of our floor mates working at the college radio station. It didn't take long for my news to hit. October 1st came up eighth, and my advisees hooted and howled as they poured me another beer and declared me "dead meat." I didn't stick around for more verbal punishment. Since it was widely predicted that anyone with a number below 135 was going to get drafted, I was numbed by my bleak options. Wanting to get away and think things through; I took a several-hour walk around Carlisle; an historic, picturesque, central Pennsylvania manufacturing town with a population somewhere around 16,000. It was a damp, cool and dreary evening, and I felt as alone as I had ever felt in my life. Since I wouldn't meet Diane until the next year, she didn't factor into my thoughts at all. My focus was only on me, and on what I was going to do. Initially, I was terribly confused, but as I strolled by stores, bars and factories, and through the poor and affluent sections of town, things gradually became obvious to me. As Quakers say, I "reached clearness."

Donn, 1970

Serving in any branch of the armed forces wasn't an option, because I'd become increasingly opposed to the war. I wasn't

going to fight, period! I also wasn't going to flee to Canada or Europe. To me, this seemed like a cowardly way out. And I wasn't going to seek some other type of deferment. I knew people who were choosing to go to divinity school, one of the few graduate deferments still available, but there was no way that I could justify that. Also, while tempted to declare myself a Conscientious Objector, at the time I wasn't certain that I was one. In spite of my previous protests to Dad, I couldn't rule out killing under all possible circumstances. So, for me, the C.O. option seemed morally corrupt. That left only one possibility. I was going to jail! I wouldn't see *Shawshank Redemption* for another twenty-five years, so my decision wasn't laced with worries over some inmate raping me. I was more concerned about how this news would go over at home. Knowing my family would have a hard time swallowing it, I hoped that they would be comforted somewhat by me being true to my convictions.

But even greater than my concern over my family's reactions was my conscious sense of being remarkably calm. My mind was made up. All seemed well. The distress of the previous few hours had evaporated. I was ready to return to the dorm, and get on with life. Making my way across town to the campus, I climbed the stairs of the dorm, and found the room where five or six of my advisees were still huddled with the blaring radio and half-filled keg. As I entered, the tipsy crew informed me that I was just in time for the "recount." Hal German, our floor's resident DJ, was about to reread the lottery results. Everyone was aware of my bad luck, and Jake Kommer, the instigator of all keg parties, began pouring beers so everyone could salute me when my birthday was read, again. Feeling older and wiser than I had a few hours earlier, it all seemed terribly juvenile to me. But I stuck around to humor the guys, and to make sure that no one fell out the window.

What followed captures the stark differences between Dad's life path as a young man and my own. Sitting on a bed sipping my beer, I waited, serenely accepting my fate, expecting to hear October 1st in the top ten. But it never happened. Hal got to 8 and read some other birthday. He got to 108, 208, 308, and still no October 1st. Finally, at three hundred and fifty-six, he announced it. Suddenly, I had as little chance of being drafted as your average Cub Scout.

I was stunned, and sat motionless on the bed. The guys, thinking it was hilarious, poured beer on me to celebrate my good luck. Wanting to know which broadcast was accurate, I called the radio station.

"Hal, this is Holtz", my nickname, "Hey, could you double check for me whether October 1st was eighth or three hundred and fifty-sixth on the lottery list."

"Sure, Holtz. No problem…Well, guess what? It's 356. Looks like you're a lottery winner. Congratulations!"

Oddly, I wasn't jubilant. Of course, I hadn't wanted to go to jail, but my confrontation with my expected fate had been spiritually profound, and it angered me that Nixon was allowing chance to whimsically dictate who would be drafted and who wouldn't. Although I was off the hook, too many others had been stamped "draftable". It all seemed so terribly wrong. Better we should all be faced with the threat of serving. Better we should all have to confront the consequences of our government's actions, and to make our own choices.

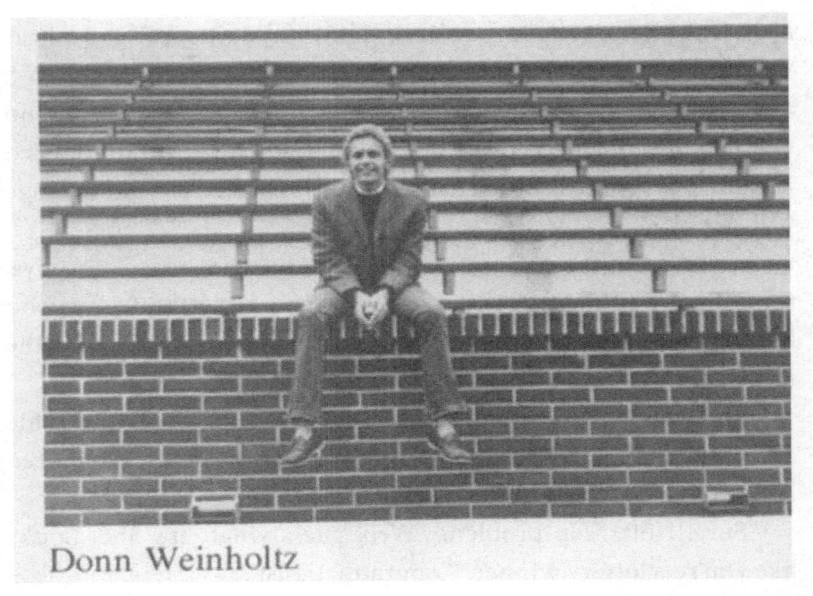

Donn's Dickinson Senior Picture at the Track

Later that semester, struggling to find a way to take a stand, I channeled my energy into opposing the war. This included quitting the college track team to march on Washington following the Cambodian invasion and Kent State slayings. Eventually, in the 1972 presidential election campaign, I canvassed door-to-door for George McGovern. But as the war continued on its own grindingly slow schedule, my life took another unexpected twist. I met Diane. Young love tempered my obsession with a morally pure response to Vietnam. I remained a staunch war opponent, but allowed myself to appreciate that I had been spared from both combat and jail. I recognized that I was a lucky guy.

On the other hand, Dad's good fortune was merely surviving the horrors of war, making it home in one piece. And even his homecoming was tragic. My grandmother's health declined substantially during the years Dad was away. She held on until he made it back; but died at home, in Dad's arms, soon after he returned.

3

GOOD YEARS

Life had conditioned Dad to be wary of what lay ahead. Although he cherished the friends and activities that he carefully selected for himself, he insulated himself from certain social situations and steeled himself for the shocks that life was sure to deliver. Drinking helped; two or three scotch on the rocks at lunch or before dinner much of the year, replaced by gin and tonics in the summer. I never heard Dad slur any words or witnessed him stagger, but we all became used to him growing louder and more emphatic when he went beyond a second drink. You didn't want to disagree with Dad at such times, and you occasionally found your self wondering how a reasonable conversation suddenly blossomed into a heated argument.

But Dad also found solace in productivity. He had the capacity to lose himself within major projects, either as an engineer designing and overseeing installation of large-scale heating and air conditioning systems or as a handyman remodeling our homes. Then, in his early forties, he took up golf. Oh my God, did he love golf; an all-consuming activity, that diverted his attention from the pressures of work, while structuring comfortable social interactions with his golf partners. The men who made up his regular foursomes over the years became his dearest friends. Others tended to be kept at a perceptible distance.

Nancy at 3 years old, 1940

Bill at 1 year old, 1940

Mom served as the great counter-balance to Dad's isolationism. By the time of their marriage, the strong-willed, flighty teenager with whom he had initially fallen in love had developed into a mature, determined women blessed with unusually good common sense and a social finesse that attracted many devoted friends. Rearing two children throughout a difficult first marriage might have been enough to sober her to life's realities; but Mom's character was forged by an additional burden during those years. At age seven, Nancy contracted polio.

Mom and Nancy, 1947

"I'll never forget it. Bill Smith and I were lying in bed one night, and Nancy called out to me from her room. She was crying and she said, 'Mommy, I can't move my legs.' It started as suddenly as that."

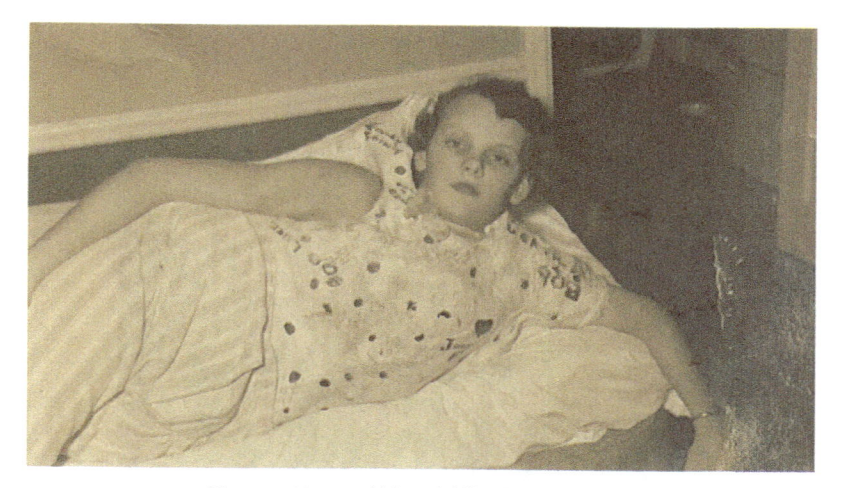

Nancy at 15 years old (1952) following spinal fusion

There followed nine years of hospitalizations and accompanying operations, necessary to save Nancy's life and to reconstruct her body. Initially, the physicians told Mom that Nancy would never walk again; but Mom assured them that Nancy would walk, and she did. In great part, Nancy's success was due to a talented Abington Hospital surgeon, Benjamin Bell, and to Abington's nursing staff under the direction of Ethel Biddle, who became a life-long, family friend known as "Aunt Ethel." But Mom was the dynamic force in Nancy's treatment plan, implementing a rigorous physical therapy regimen involving endless hours of massage and exercise. Mom's younger sister, Aunt Mary, once told me: "Your mother would stand on one side of the room, and Nancy would be lying on the floor on the other side. Gada would insist that Nancy crawl across the room to her, and Nancy would try; but she would have so much trouble, and she would start to cry. I'd be watching, and I'd be feeling so sorry for her. I'd want her to be able to call it a day, but Gada wouldn't let her quit. She'd stand there, and her voice would get a little edge in it. And she'd tell Nancy that she couldn't do anything else that day, until she had finished crossing that room."

Nancy and Bill, 1946

    Mom's "tough love" approach was a remarkable success. Even though Nancy would always have a noticeable limp and a visibly distorted back; she walked without braces, and even played goalie for her high school field hockey team. Furthermore, Nancy never revealed the slightest indication of being impaired in any way. She came through her ordeal a fiercely determined, but fun loving, young woman, who attracted legions of male and female friends. Of course, none of these outcomes were obvious when Nancy was eleven and Mom married Dad. But Nancy's struggles became their struggles, her victories, their victories; and her life an omen of what was to follow. Mom and Dad had a wonderful run of forty-five years. Dad became the vice-president of a small heating and air conditioning company, and later became an associate in a major Philadelphia architectural firm. Mom assumed the role of socially active housewife; running our home and controlling all aspects of the family budget, while volunteering heavily for the March of Dimes and the United Fund. We lived much of that time in comfortable suburban Philadelphia, always summering in Ocean City. After I went away to college, Mom and Dad moved year-round to Ocean City, where they stayed for five years, until Dad's retirement. Then it was on to a condominium in Stuart, Florida for the final sixteen years of their lives.

Granny, Grandfather George Larsen and Mom, 1915

My grandmother, Mary Christensen ("Granny"), stayed with them right up until she died in Ocean City, at eighty-nine. Nancy and Bill both married and moved out of the house before I was a teenager. Nancy lived in NewYork, Ohio and New Jersey, but returned home to live with us when her first marriage to Dick Hornbaker ended, as I was turning sixteen. Her children, Lynn and Scott, who were ten and twelve years younger than me, were like my younger brother and sister. Just as I was finishing college, Nancy and the kids moved out when Nancy married her second husband, Al ("Bub") Flanagan. Throughout, Bill stayed close by with his five boys (Billy, Randy, Kris, Terry and K.C.), adding the three additional children (David, Ray and Nina) when he and Edie married.

Lynn, 1963

Scott, 1963

    Their willingness to have Nancy, Lynn and Scott move home with us showed how Mom and Dad were exceptionally supportive of us all. We had four generations living in one household, and they were always there when needed. While there are too many examples to cite them all, their approach during my grandmother's declining years may be the single best illustration of Mom and Dad's devotion to family.

    The fact that Granny lived with us at all made our family an anomaly. Remarkably few people my age had live-in grandmothers. But I knew no other way, and Granny contributed much to our home. She did all the laundry and some of the cooking; and she babysat for me every Saturday night, while Mom and Dad went out. In fact, when I was a child Granny and I were steady companions. Together, we watched countless Phillies' games and we played endless hands of pinochle, while the Perry Como Show or The Saturday Night Movie provided background entertainment on Granny's, bedroom, color TV.

Nancy and Granny (1972) at Diane and Donn's Wedding

We'll never know whether or not Granny suffered from Alzheimer's Disease, the diagnosis was rarely made in the early 70's. We were told that she suffered from "senility" due to decreased blood flow to the brain. A substantial decline in her alertness and attitude was clear as early as 1967, my first year of college. When Diane met Granny in 1970, she was just a shell of her former self. By then she spent much of her time sitting in a chair gazing off across the room; barely responding if you talked to her, but often calling for Mom to provide her help, of some sort, whenever she needed it. During the last year or so, Granny spent increasing amounts of time in bed, where she would lie staring at the ceiling, periodically groaning aloud. When we visited at her last Christmas, Granny was so unresponsive that we weren't sure if she was hearing anything we said. Diane and I bought her a stained-glass, fruit mobile that we hung directly over her in the hope that it might provide her some pleasure. A few weeks later, in her final night at home, Granny experienced excruciating pain. Mom and Dad called her physician, who recommended that an ambulance take her to the hospital. She died within twenty-four hours.

Aunt Mary (date unknown)

Granny could easily have been relegated to a nursing home, but Mom wouldn't allow it. She somehow always managed to find sitters to attend to Granny, while she took breaks for shopping or socializing with friends. Mom even navigated her way through her own health crisis, a bout of breast cancer, including a radical mastectomy, without too greatly disturbing Granny's routine. If Dad complained, after a third drink, it was only that he was concerned about the burden on Mom. Dad usually found external targets for his frustrations. As Mom confided to me, around the time of Mom's operation, he lashed out at Aunt Mary, who lived two-hours away and had the primary responsibility for her ailing father-in-law, for not helping more with "her own mother." Dad's attack added to an already palpable tension between him and Aunt Mary, who also got loud and feisty after a few drinks; but their little tempest was the only conflict that I recall around the potentially difficult issue of Granny's care. One of the few times that I ever saw Mom cry was at the family viewing that we had just before Granny's funeral. Though smiling, as usual, Mom couldn't hold back the tears as she spoke to the funeral director.

"You know she lived with us for over thirty years. I realize that it's a blessing that she doesn't have to suffer any more, but it's still awfully hard to say goodbye to an old friend."

By the time that Granny died, Diane and I had been married for over three years; having wed immediately after Diane's December, 1972 graduation from Dickinson. We moved to Chapel Hill, North Carolina in October of 1973 soon after I completed a Master's Degree and received my social studies teacher certification from Shippensburg State College. Diane was already a certified science teacher and we applied to the Peace-Corps in hope of teaching in Africa, Latin America or Asia. However, the Peace Corps informed us that they could place Diane, but they had nothing for a humanities "generalist" like me. Also, at the time there was a teacher glut in the U.S., and neither of us could find a teaching position, anywhere. So, we opted for a move to Chapel Hill when I accepted an offer to be a college "traveler" (textbook salesman) for Harper and Row Publishers, and was assigned the North Carolina territory. I wasn't thrilled with going into sales; but I figured that at least I would be doing something connected to education, we'd get to move to an interesting place, and we wouldn't have to keep waitressing and bartending, as we'd been doing over the summer while waiting for our Peace Corps and teaching application rejections.

Soon after we arrived in Chapel Hill, Diane found a job at a cancer research lab at Duke University, but within a year we both quit our jobs and accepted positions at Chapel Hill High School; where in addition to our teaching, Diane coached girls soccer and I coached boys and girls cross country and track. Diane continued teaching the entire seven years that we lived in the Chapel Hill area, and she also completed a Master's Degree in Science Education at the University of North Carolina. (Fifteen years later she finished a Ph.D. in the same area at the University of Connecticut.) Meanwhile, I left high school teaching and obtained a Ph.D. in Adult andHigher Education from UNC. I was attracted to my graduate program because it gave me the opportunity to study group dynamics applied to classroom teaching and school management. After about a year of coursework, I was offered a fellowship in the educational research and development office at UNC's School of Medicine. While there, I found a niche for myself by focusing my dissertation research on the teaching done by the university medical faculty serving as attending physicians on hospital wards. The teams of residents, interns and medical students overseen and taught by the "attendings" were naturally occurring, small groups working and learning in a fast-paced, demanding setting. Though exhausting, the dissertation turned into a rewarding project and something of a ground-breaking study, eventually leading to job offers in other medical schools. Getting a job suddenly became top priority because, while I was still gathering my dissertation data, Diane became pregnant with David. We decided that Diane was going to leave teaching for a year after our baby was born, and my graduate school fellowship didn't pay enough to support three of us. So, we desperately needed me to come up with full-time employment. Given my experience in medical education, I had no trouble getting interviews for great positions in medical schools; but in spite of submitting endless applications for other academic jobs, nobody showed any interest in me. So, with David due in a few months, I accepted a position at the University of Texas Medical Branch in Galveston.

Three weeks after David was born, we sent all of our belongings and our dog, Ebony, to Galveston in a moving van, while we flew to Texas. Mom and Dad, who had driven from Florida, met us at Houston Intercontinental Airport. It was comforting to have Mom and Dad waiting for us, but on the two-hour drive to Galveston, I felt unsettled. It was so hot and humid outside. The sprawl of Houston was daunting. A radio spot warning about taking proper precautions during Hurricane season was worrisome. Things just weren't "right."

I had visited Galveston twice. The first time was for an intensive round of interviews. The second time Diane went with me to search for a house. I'd enjoyed both trips; but now, moving with our three-week-old baby, the stark differences between Chapel Hill and the Texas Gulf Coast were overwhelming. As we arrived in Galveston, I thought, "Geez, I think I made a big mistake." But I didn't dare say a word to anyone. To my great relief, I felt a lot better once we reached our house.

We had purchased a small, Victorian, two-story model in Galveston's historic East End. The neighborhood was beautiful, consisting primarily of stately older homes that had survived the Great Galveston Hurricane of 1900. Ours was only a half-mile from the medical school, so I could either bike or walk to work.

Mom and Dad

Mom and Dad spent two weeks helping us get settled in. Their visit was a lot of fun. Mom tirelessly unpacked and helped to decorate. She loved that kind of thing. Dad was also a big help. He installed two ceiling fans, and he built a small workbench for my tools. We went out for dinner a few times, and Dad and I played the two local golf courses. Their visit was topped off by hours of watching baseball as the Phillies won the 1980 World Series; fulfilling a lifelong dream of mine. But things quickly took a downward turn. Even though my medical school boss, Harold Levine, was wonderfully supportive as I learned how to evaluate the basic science curriculum, Diane and I never adjusted to Galveston's climate; virtually no winter, chronic high humidity, and hurricane threats five months a year. Within a few months, Harold and his wife, Paula, lost a major portion of their roof to a waterspout that unexpectedly came ashore one night. Soon afterwards, a "minor" tropical depression generated fourteen inches of rain and spawned five tornadoes that touched down within a mile of our house. As Diane, David, Ebony and I huddled in a small living room closet during the height of the storm, I thought that maybe I should start looking for another job. Various other factors contributed to my desire to bail out. For example, the bugs were awful. There was that large tree roach that I found in the bottom of my iced tea glass, one evening; as well as the others that raced around Ebony's dog food bowl when I turned on the kitchen light, late at night. Also, the fleas were so bad that I was forced to spray the entire yard, and under the house, every month, year-round. We had a great little, fenced-in yard, but we couldn't let David crawl around in the grass because of the pesticide.

And there was the crime. A drunken man nearly ran us down in his car as we pushed David's stroller, on our first afternoon walking on the beach. The East End Rapist attacked multiple victims, in their homes, on our side of town. Two separate drunks drove their cars up on neighbors' lawns. A man snatched another neighbor's purse in front of her house. Two guys terrorized a couple at knife point in their apartment, just a block away from us. And a male and female duo kidnapped a child at a nearby playground. All of this happened within one year. It was mind boggling.

As the bizarre events continually piled up , our whole situation seemed more and more troubling. But we kept adapting and coping. Diane's father designed and installed a sensitive and startlingly, loud alarm system for our house. And Diane and I organized an effective block watch and female escort program. We were hanging in there. Then came the last straw. Following a bitter dispute with an associate dean, Harold lost his position as director of our office, although he maintained a tenured faculty position elsewhere in the medical school. I sided with Harold, but as a recently hired, untenured faculty member, I was in a precarious position. On top of everything else, with my work setting now in turmoil, I was certain that it was time to exit.

But in our short amount of time in Galveston, we had made many good friends, and Diane had just accepted a teaching position at a local parochial school. So, she didn't immediately share my enthusiasm for moving.

Even though it entailed a substantial pay cut, when it looked like I might be able to land a joint appointment in the Colleges of Education and Medicine at the University of Iowa, I went into high gear trying to convince Diane that we should go.

"Honey, we've got to make the jump now, or we'll get trapped here. Texas pays so much more than other places that we'll end up being sucked in by the money."

"But, Donn, we just got here. Let's just stay for a few more years. You'll have other opportunities further east. We can go then. Besides, I just took this job, and I know that I'm really going to like it. I enjoy being with the nuns, and the school is so peaceful! If I hadn't met you, I think that I could have liked living in a convent."

"Well, thanks for choosing me. But look, I may have other offers from medical schools, but I might never get another shot at having my primary appointment in a school of education. It's almost too good to be true, Diane. Iowa City is a beautiful university town. You'll love it, and you'll get another teaching job. You'll always get job offers because you are the best!"

"You'll be closer to Katherine." (Diane's best friend in high school, who had settled in Vincennes, Indiana.) "I promise that we'll go to see her a couple of times a year. And we'll be able to drive home to Philly and New Jersey instead of flying. It will save us a lot of money, and we can afford to go home more often!"

"Are you sure it's closer to Katherine?"

Aha! By Diane's voice, I knew that the "Katherine" appeal had tipped things in Iowa's favor.

"Of course, I'm sure!"

"Show me on a map."

I got out a road atlas, and turned to the map of the United States. To get to Vincennes from Iowa City you had to travel east for about fifty miles, cross the Mississippi River, and angle south/southeast across Illinois. Then, once you reached Indiana, you'd head directly south for another fifty miles. The whole trip looked like it would take five to six hours, depending on how hard you traveled.

"That doesn't look close to me!"

"Well, I never said that it was real close. But it's a hell of a lot closer than it is from here, and if we stay put you'll practically never get to see Katherine."

"Do you promise that we'll visit her regularly?"

"Not every month, but a couple of times a year. I swear on it!"

"But we'll still be nowhere near New Jersey or Philadelphia."

"Good point. It's about eleven hundred miles, but that's still only a two-day drive, which is a lot cheaper than flying home from here."

"OK, you can keep talking to them, and I'll think about it."

I got the offer, and could start in mid-October; but Diane still didn't cave in easily.

"We'll go, but I want to be able to concentrate on my teaching right up until we leave. It is bad enough that I'll be quitting after six weeks. I want to make sure that I do a really good job. The nuns are so nice!"

"It's a deal. I'll do all the packing." (Iowa not only paid less, they refused to pay any moving expenses.)

"You won't have to do a thing."

"Sure I won't!"

"No, I guarantee it. I'll pack everything. When do you want to fly up and look for a house?"

"I want you to fly up and buy a house. It will be cheaper, and I won't be distracted from my job."

"Come on! You've got to come along to choose the house."

"Nope. We've already gotten two houses, and you know what I like. You can do it for us. I trust your taste."

"OK. I'll buy the house."

And I did. And I also packed two or three boxes a day over a month and a half. Then, a few days after an evening, good-bye picnic on the beach, all of our friends helped us load the U-Haul.

The next morning, we put David in a car seat between us, Ebony in the Toyota that we were towing behind us, and we headed across the causeway away from Galveston Island. We passed Houston, and veered north to the great midwest. All the while, a hurricane was churning away in the middle of the Gulf. At the time, we didn't know if it would veer towards Galveston or not (it didn't); but with each mile we drove, I savored the fact that it wasn't going to hit us.

Coralville, IA house

Three days later, we pulled into Coralville, the town immediately adjacent to Iowa City, where I had purchased our house; and once again, Mom and Dad were waiting for us. They had arrived several days earlier, whereupon Dad parked himself in the basement, so he could "supervise" the contractor who was taking out our humongous, old oil furnace and replacing it with a smaller, more efficient one. When, over the phone, Dad shared his intentions of doing this, I was worried that the contractor would be bothered by Dad looking over his shoulder the entire time. But I was dead wrong. The fellow was semi-retired and quite friendly. He and Dad hit it off just fine. By the time that we arrived, the two of them had already gotten in one round of golf and they were making plans for another.

Mom and Dad

Meanwhile, Mom had purchased curtains and kitchen utensils, and begun cleaning. It was a new location, but it was "déjà vu' all over again." I had about two weeks before I had to actually start my job, so there was plenty of time to work on the house, get settled in, and become oriented to the area. Again, mixing the work with dinners out, golf and shopping, we had a great time. For years, I shuddered at the thought of ever moving again; but I knew that if we ever needed to, we could count on Mom and Dad to help make it happen.

Iowa City was a wonderful place for us. Despite its distance from major urban centers, it's a surprisingly cosmopolitan and fun town because the University of Iowa draws a large number of students from all over the world. The Colleges of Education and Medicine, where I worked, provided me with solid professional experience, and the friendships that we developed with my colleagues and students and their families were deeply rewarding. Also, as predicted, in spite of sharp competition Diane quickly landed a biology teaching job at Iowa City's City High School, where she felt as positive about her job and co-workers as I did about mine. Particularly helpful was the school district's willingness to allow Diane to cut back to half-time when Philip was born, three years after we arrived. Finally, our friendships with our neighbors in Coralville and with the members of the Quaker Meeting in nearby West Branch were truly special to us. By practically every measure imaginable, we had the complete package.

There were only two glitches, one minor and one major. The minor one was caused by my own peculiar topography fetish. Both Diane and I love trees and mountains, but in their absence, I become pretty obsessive about needing them. Although Eastern Iowa, due to the effects of ice-age glaciation, has more rolling hills than most Americans realize, there are no large forests and the nearest mountains are a long day's drive away. Furthermore, all of Iowa, though "rural", is so dedicated to food production that no sizable "wild areas" of any kind exist. Where they can be found, they are beautiful, but by my standards, exquisite miniatures. I came to think of them as "pocket parks." When exploring many of these parks, we always seemed to be within a mile's walk of large cornfields. At first this was no problem for me because there is real beauty and serenity in panoramas of cornfields, but once I became fully aware of the extent to which the fields were doused with herbicides and pesticides, I couldn't shake the imagery of the state as one big "agri-factory."

Family Hike

In our hikes through the picturesque little parks, Diane could always lose herself in the beauty of the location immediately surrounding her, but not me.

"Honey. This is a wonderful spot, but look, over there. Cornfields! What did I tell you! We had to bump into them sooner or later. Here we are, again, on a small wilderness island, surrounded by a giant sea of corn growing in Lorsban (insecticide) soaked soil."

"Donn, can't you just enjoy what we have?"

"Nope. I try. Believe me I try. There are so many things that I love about Iowa. But I can't let this go."

"Oh my, you're not neurotic about many things, but when you are…!"

My fixation was magnified by our occasional jaunts to places like theSawtooth Mountains in Idaho, to visit Diane's sister Susan and her husband (at the time) Frank at their summer cabin; as well as our regular treks to Philadelphia and New Jersey. Crossing through Pennsylvania with its vast tracts of trees and scenic mountains really did it to me. Upon reaching the Pennsylvania turnpike, a warm feeling would envelope me, and I would invariably utter something ridiculous.

"If only Iowa butted up against Pennsylvania! I wish that I could just find a way to eliminate Ohio, Indiana and Illinois. I mean really! There ought to be some way to engineer this."

All of that distance that I wished would magically disappear was also the source of our more serious problem. We were still living too far from our families. It took too long to drive to Philly, Jersey or Florida to see them. And we couldn't afford to fly.

Not that we didn't make the trips! We went to Florida to visit Mom and Dad every spring break for a week, and we drove to Philadelphia and North or South Jersey two or three times a year, including Christmas. It was hard enough covering a thousand miles or more, one-way, with one child in the car, but by the time we got to three it was a peculiar form of hell; especially when slogging through three distinct winter storm tracks, or dodging summer tornadoes.

Mom on the front steps with Diane, David and Philip

Mom and Dad came out to Iowa each year to visit for about two weeks, and Diane's parents, Dick and Jane Thistle, drove out twice a year for a week at a time. But those arrangements couldn't hold up over the long haul. With both sets of parents getting older, their ability to make the journey was time-limited. Also, with most of our aunts and uncles being older than our parents, we were facing drop-of-the-hat trips back home for funerals. There was no way around these problems, and they began to eat away at me. The discomfort was never terrible; but sometime around our fourth year in Iowa I began feeling the nagging dissonance of knowing that, even though our family was remarkably content, we wouldn't be staying.

As usual, I did my best to relieve my frustration by trying to make the impossible happen. I began lobbying for our families to move to Iowa. But this was spitting in the wind. Mom and Dad were happy as clams in Florida, and Diane's folks weren't going to be cajoled into leaving their New Jersey home of thirty years. I'd bring up the subject to Diane's dad, extolling the virtues of Iowa City and pointing out that he and Diane's mom would be able to see the boys—at the time their only grandchildren—whenever they wanted. Once, Dad Thistle shot back:

"Yeah, sure. As often as you move, we'd get out there, and you'd be off to another job. You'd probably end up back east somewhere!"

"But, Dad, we've got great jobs now. There's no reason to move again. All that we need to really round things out is to have one set of parents out here. That would do the trick. No further moves. I promise!"

Laughing at me, he replied, "Donn, I couldn't make you promise that. What if a wonderful opportunity came along? Then you would have to pass it up. How would that sit with you?"

Donn, Dad Thistle, Diane and David

He had me. Even though I kept insisting that I could stay put the rest of my life, I hadn't considered the possibility of an alluring offer from out of the blue. Since I had always chased hard after my jobs, nothing like that had ever happened to me; but it might. It wasn't impossible. So, at that point I consciously conceded. Although with both families I continued jokingly bringing up the topic of us someday all being happy in Iowa, we all knew that I was just dusting off an old joke.

I was really in no position to complain because Diane and I had initially triggered the distance dilemma by moving to North Carolina; which, in turn, helped Mom and Dad decide to move to Florida. They had fully intended to retire to Ocean City. However, after Diane and I were settled in Chapel Hill for a while, they began quietly considering the move to Stuart, on Florida's east coast, about 50 miles north of Palm Beach.

Some of their friends had retired to Stuart, and for a few years Mom and Dad drove down from New Jersey to see us each February, and continued on to Stuart for a two-week vacation. Then, all of a sudden, they announced that they had bought a condominium at Vista Del Lago, an adult community in Stuart's north end, and they immediately put the house in Ocean City up for sale. This was particularly distressing news for Nancy, Bill, me and our families, who were all deeply attached to Ocean City. Diane and I had planned to eventually move much closer to Philadelphia in order to be near both of our families. But as Mom bluntly told me:

"Donn, we can't plan our whole lives around the possibility that you might return someday. It's costly keeping up this big house, and it's much more than we need. Your father doesn't have a pension plan, so we are going to have to live off of our savings, social security, and what we can make on the sale of the house. The difference between the cost of the condominium and what we can get for this isn't going to be huge, but it will make for a nice nest egg. It will help a lot later on."

So, Mom and Dad moved, and then we moved to Texas, and then on to Iowa. Like so many far-flung American families we had to adjust to being spread out across the country. For a few summers, Nancy and Bub and Mom and Dad jointly rented a place in Ocean City, and the rest of us visited them. Then Nancy and Bub bought the place next door to Mom and Dad's old house, and we got together there in the summer; as well as having Christmas Eve at Nancy and Bub's home in Philadelphia. These trips east, which always included visits with Diane's family, along with our annual trips to Florida, an occasional trip to Idaho, and our parents' sojourns to visit us, managed to keep both extended families reasonably connected. The phone bills got pretty expensive, and we logged horrendous numbers of miles on our cars. It could be very tiring, but somehow it all worked. We held together.

4

MISSING

At 1:00 P.M. on Thursday, January 12, 1995, I walked into a conference room at the Connecticut State Department of Higher Education, and eased into a seat next to Chuck Case, the Dean of Education at the University of Connecticut. For three and one-half years, I had been Dean of Education, Nursing and Health Professions at the University of Hartford, and along with other education deans from around the state, I was attending a meeting to discuss ways that we might collaborate on reforming our teacher education programs. Chuck knew that my mother had died the previous spring, and with older parents of his own, I knew that he would lend a sympathetic ear.

"Hey, Donn, how are you doing?"

"Hi, Chuck. To tell you the truth, I'm a little on edge right now."

"What's the matter?"

"My Dad is getting off the Auto Train in Florida, probably at this very minute, and I'm concerned about him driving home. It's a three-hour trip, and he's nearly eighty-one years old. He had a stroke a few years ago, and he can't drive the way he used to."

"Whew! Hold your breath. I know what you are going through."

I was seriously worried. Of course, Dad had refused my offer to drive him down to Lorton to catch the Auto Train. But, at the last minute, he had agreed to having Billy and his brother, Ray, take him. My two nephews dropped him off around noon on Wednesday, January 11. The train was loading when they arrived, so they said a quick good-bye, leaving Dad in line in his car; and went into a neighboring restaurant to catch a bite to eat before heading back to Philadelphia. When they came out of the restaurant, the train had departed. It would be about twenty-four hours before it arrived in Sanford, just outside of Orlando.

I figured that, before calling, I would give Dad plenty of time to make the trip to Stuart, have some dinner, and get settled in at home. David had a recreational league basketball practice that night; so as usual, I drove him to the gym and watched. When we got home, it was around 9:00 P.M. Hoping that Dad would be parked by his television by then, I dialed his number. There was no answer.

"I was afraid of this." I called Bill immediately.

"I know, Donn. I didn't get an answer either. I wonder what's up."

"I don't know. He should have been there by now. He wouldn't stay late at the Olive Garden after a long trip like that, and I don't think that he would stop to see Aunt Ruth. Maybe he's spending the night at a motel. He probably didn't sleep all night."

"Yeah, but you'd think that he would call."

"Well, hopefully he still will, but it's getting kind of late. Listen, if we don't hear something from him by tomorrow, we'll have to shift into high gear to try to find him."

"OK, let's hope for the best. I'll talk to you tomorrow night." Bill and I both went to work on Friday, and each of us repeatedly tried to get in touch with Dad. Bill had an 800-line at work, so he called Stuart over a dozen times without getting an answer. I waited until about 1:30 P.M. and began calling every hour with the same result. At 4:30, I had an appointment with Anne Fitzmaurice, the Interim Vice President for Academic Affairs at the University of Hartford. Although we met for nearly an hour, my mind wasn't on the meeting at all. It was racing through all the things that might have gone wrong, and what we might do in response to them. At 5:30, I returned to my office, called Dad's apartment once again, and then tried the Olive Garden. No one there had seen him. So, I tried Aunt Ruth.

"Well, Donn, that is unusual. He certainly should have been here by now. Especially your father. You know he's not the type to go out of his way and do something unexpectedly. I hope that he is alright."

"Yeah, I know, Aunt Ruth. This isn't like him at all. I've got to call Bill. I'll be back in touch as soon as I know something more."

"Please do, Donn; and thanks for letting me know. I'll keep a lookout, and if he shows up, I'll have him give you a call right away."

"Thanks Aunt Ruth. It really helps to have you there." I drove home first, and then I called Bill. We decided to turn to the police, and we worked out an initial plan. Bill would call the Florida Highway Patrol, while I would call the Sanford Police. Diane, the kids and I had been planning on going to Cape Cod for the weekend. Although it was the middle of winter, we had wanted to go to the Cape because, even though we'd been living in New England for several years, we'd never managed to get out there to see what it was like. So much for that plan! Diane called and canceled our motel reservations.

When I talked to the Sanford Police, the officer I spoke to explained to me that he couldn't do anything unless it was definite that Dad was actually missing in the area. He said that the first step in verifying that would be for me to call Amtrak to see if Dad and his car had arrived in Florida. If they hadn't, this would be a case for the police in Lorton, Virginia. So, I called the Amtrak office in Sanford about 7:30 P.M., but the office was closed. There was a recording with a number for Amtrak National, so I called it. The person who answered transferred me to Amtrak Police, who verified that Dad and his car had left Lorton on the train, but they couldn't tell me if he had collected the car in Sanford. I would have to wait until morning, when the Sanford office opened, in order to find out. Bill had made a bit more progress with the Florida Highway Patrol. They put a bulletin out to all of their stations to be on the lookout for Dad, but it was clear that there would be no active search launched immediately. We had reached the end of our options for the day, and would have to wait until the rest of the world assumed their work stations on Saturday before we could push ahead any further. Given our increasing panic, it was a hard fact to swallow.

I couldn't sleep that night. The national news had recently focused on a series of murders at Florida highway rest stops, and I was haunted by the possibility that Dad had been mugged and left somewhere to die. His recently purchased car, a loaded Mercury sedan, might appeal to a car thief, and Dad was an easy target. My mental images kept changing all night long, but they were all horrible. At one point, I dozed off only to awaken with a start after dreaming that Dad was tied up in the trunk of the car, which had been stripped and ditched in a swamp. My soul ached at the prospect.

"He's already been through too much in life! He deserves a better ending!"

Sensing that I was completely losing control, I pleaded with myself.

"This is hell, but get a hold of yourself! Too many other things could have happened. He might even be ok. Don't lose it yet. Take this one day at a time, and just get through tomorrow."

Central FL

Sanford, FL[1]

When morning finally arrived, I called Amtrak in Sanford, and found out that Dad had collected his car.[1] So, I called the Sanford Police, only to be told that they could do nothing more than alert

---

1. Images generated through Google Maps. https://maps.app.goo.gl/HzVv46N5Dew688ig7

police stations throughout Florida to be on the lookout. The officer in Sanford suggested that I call the Martin County Sheriff, who has jurisdiction over Stuart, in case Dad had been spotted closer to home. Upon doing so, I was told that we had to physically verify that Dad was not at his apartment in order to commence a missing person search. I was relieved when they were willing to send a deputy over to Vista Del Lago to meet Aunt Ruth, obtain her key, and check Dad's apartment. But after the deputy conducted the search, he informed me that he couldn't take a missing person report from Aunt Ruth because she was not a family member, and he also could-n't take it from me over the phone. He told me to call Sanford again, because that was the last place that Dad had been seen. When I did, the Sanford police told me to call Lorton, Virginia, since that was the last place that Dad had been seen by family members.

The run-a-round was maddening, but I was too worried about wasting valuable time to get angry and vent at anyone. We needed the missing person report to trigger an interstate alert and FBI cooperation. I pushed on and called Lorton.

"I'm sorry, sir. I'll talk to my supervisor, but I'm sure that I can't take your report over the phone. Your nephews will have to drive over here."

"But they're in Philadelphia!"

"I can't send an officer up there. Maybe they can file with their local police, since that is the last place your father stayed."

"That's ok. I don't expect you to send anybody up there. I'm just getting upset at not being able to file a report over the phone. We'll try inPennsylvania. Thanks for your help."

At that point, I called Bill, explained the whole exasperating sequence of events, and asked him to call the Lower Gwynned (Pa.) police to see if they would complete the missing person report. After we hung up, I called Aunt Ruth again to see about identifying Dad's credit cards so we could put a trace on them. The idea had come to me in the middle of the night, probably because I had recently been following the case of a missing Connecticut school superintendent whose whereabouts had been determined this way. I remembered Mom telling me that she had registered with a credit card hot line. So, I figured that Aunt Ruth could look around in Mom's and Dad's financial records (in Mom's desk in the den) and maybe come up with the hot line telephone number.

Bingo! Aunt Ruth was able to locate the number a few minutes after she entered the apartment. She immediately called me with the information, and I called the hot line. After I explained our situation, they asked me a series of questions, including Mom's birthday and Granny's maiden name, to determine if I was legitimate. Once they were convinced that I was ok, they told me that since 1977 Mom and Dad had listed eight credit cards with their service: four gas cards, a Citibank Visa, an American Express card and a few department store cards. They also provided 800 numbers to call for all the cards. Soon after I hung up, Bill called me back.

"Our police department was very helpful, and they took the report over the phone."

"You're kidding."

Nope. They didn't make any issue about it, at all."

"Jesus, I guess that it varies from state to state."

"Maybe so. Anyway, they'll alert the FBI who should put out some sort of inter-state bulletin."

"Good job, Bill. I finally feel like we're starting to make some head-way."

"Yeah. Hey, they also said that we should go down and sort throughDad's things to find out what credit cards he has. That way we can put a trace on them."

"I've already got them!"

"How'd you do that?"

"Psychic I guess."

I explained about the hot line, and we agreed to distribute the credit card calls between us. Bill would start with Citibank and Sunoco, and I would try American Express and Mobil.

Having been on the phone the entire morning, I was feeling blitzed. At Diane's urging, I took a break to get something to eat. Before I finished my sandwich, Bill called.

"We've got a bite!"

"Great. What's the scoop?"

"Citibank says that they authorized use of Dad's credit card at a Holiday Inn in Florida."

"Alright! Where in Florida?"

"I don't know. She couldn't tell me."

"What do you mean? That's crazy. They've got to know."
"You'd think so, but she claims not. All she knows is that they cleared use of the card at a Holiday Inn somewhere in Florida."
"Well, I guess that we start calling every Holiday Inn between Sanford and Stuart. That shouldn't be all that hard."

"Yeah, listen, I'll call the Holiday Inn here in Ft. Washington and find out if they can tell me the names of the Holiday Inns around Sanford. At least we have a lead!"

"OK. I'll wait to hear from you."

While Bill tried to track down the Florida locations through his local Holiday Inn, I pulled out our road atlas and peered at the Sanford-Orlando area. Then, on impulse, I decided to call 1-800-Holiday to see what I could turn up. When the operator answered, I briefly explained our dilemma and asked her for the names of the Holiday Inns closest to Sanford. She was very helpful.

"Well, there is no longer one in Sanford. It closed down, and there are thirty-five within a reasonable drive of Orlando."

"My God! Then just give me the names of the one's that are closest to Sanford. We might as well start with them."

"The three closest are Altamonte, Winter Park and Arena. Here are the numbers that you can call…. And good luck. I hope that you locate your father very soon."

"Thanks. I really appreciate your help."

I called Altamonte.

"No, your father didn't check in here, but I think that I may have just talked to your brother."

Figuring that I had better stop duplicating his efforts, I called Bill. He was excited.

"Donn! Citibank just called me. They say the charge was from Sanford, but they're still not sure from where. There was a Holiday Inn there, but it closed."

"Yeah, I know. I did some calling on my own. I found out from 1-800-Holiday. Do you suppose that charges from whatever replaced the Holiday Inn are still registering as "Holiday Inn"?

"I don't know. Could be. Let's try to find out what went in there." "OK. Let's divide up the area Holiday Inns and see what they can tell us." "Sounds good, and I'll call that 800-Holiday number and see if they can tell me anything more."

"Who needs the FBI. We'll find the old boy ourselves!"

"You bet!"

Things were starting to break our way. We were both on an adrenaline high. I quickly dialed the Arena Holiday Inn, which I assumed was near the home of the Orlando Magic. The desk clerk was sincerely concerned, but she couldn't offer much help.

"I'm really not sure. I know that it closed about a year ago, but I don't know if anything replaced it…"

"Well, if the franchise did change, do you think that a recent charge could show up at Citibank as 'Holiday Inn'?"

"I really don't think so. I've never heard of anything like that before."

"I know. It sounds strange to me too, but that's what I'm hoping happened. Thanks for your help."

I had hung up for only a few seconds when the phone rang. It was Bill."I found him!"

"Thank God! Where is he?"

"He's at Central Regional Hospital in Sanford. He was staying at the Marina Inn in Sanford, which was the old Holiday Inn."

(The first place that Bill had called had been able to tell him the Marina Inn's name.) "He checked in there on Thursday complaining that he was tired and had a bad cold. Apparently, he just stayed in bed and kept ordering room service. He spent Friday night too. Then he went to the desk this morning to register for a third night. Kristin, the desk clerk that I just talked to, thought that he looked so bad that she called 911 for an ambulance. They came, picked him up, and took him to the hospital just a few hours ago."

"Did you talk to him?"

Holiday Inn-Marina Inn, Sanford, FL[2]

"Nope. Not yet. I called the hospital, and they confirmed that he is there and that he is stable, but he doesn't have a room with a phone yet. I think that you ought to call. You're the one who knows your way around hospitals."[2]

"No problem. I'll call right away and see what I can find out. But, Jesus, did he seem sick when he left your place?"

"Not at all. He did complain about a runny nose, but I hardly saw him blow it at all, and he wasn't coughing or anything. If he was, we wouldn't have let him leave."

---

2. Ping, D. (2016, August 2). *City staff reviewing Marina Island alf*. Sanford, Fla. https://thebokey.com/2016/08/02/city-staff-reviewing-marina-island-alf/

"It must have flared up on him in no time while he was on the train. He might have come down with one of those virulent pneumonia strains like the one that killed Jim Henson." (The creator of The Muppets) At Dad's age, he'd hardly have any resistance at all."

"Maybe. But at least now we've found him. Hopefully they'll be able to patch him up, and he can go home in a few days."

"Yeah, I hope so. Great job, Bill!"

"You too. We did it together."

"We did do pretty good didn't we. Maybe we ought to go into the tracking missing persons business. I can see it: 'We'll find your friend or loved one in less than twenty-four hours. It's guaranteed!' How about it?"

"Maybe after I retire."

"OK, we'll wait! In the meantime, I'll call the hospital and see what's up."

Central Regional Hospital in Sanford, FL[3]

Before calling Central Regional, I dialed the Marina Inn and thanked Kristin for her help. She was very concerned about Dad.[3]

"He was so sweet. He didn't want to bother anybody, and he kept saying that he would get better once he had enough orange juice and sleep. But by this morning he could barely talk over the

---

3. Solutions, H. W. (2022). *Central Florida Regional Hospital.* ENGAGE. https://engage.healthtrustjobs.com/facility-spotlights/central-florida-regional-hospital

phone, and I finally did get him to acknowledge that maybe he should see a doctor. Then he walked down here to register for tonight, and he could hardly stand. He sat down in a chair in the lobby and began coughing horribly. That's when I called the ambulance. I'm so glad that they got him to the hospital. Please tell him that I hope that he gets well soon."

I assured her that I would, and I hung up. Within a few minutes I got a call from another motel employee, a woman named Martha, who assured me that they would lock up Dad's wallet and car keys until he, or some family member, came to claim them. I thanked her, and immediately called the hospital, before I could be interrupted by another phone call. Through a stroke of good fortune, I was immediately able to reach Dad.

"Hi,...Donn. I'm...in...the...hospital. I...can't...talk...now. They're getting ready...to move....me...to a different....room."

He was very weak and groggy.

"That's alright, Dad. We're all just so relieved to know where you are, and that you are OK. Let me talk to one of the nurses now, and I'll talk to you as soon as you are in your new room."

"Sure enough,....Donn....Thanks....for calling."

I briefly spoke to a nurse who explained to me that Dad was not going to Intensive Care, but rather to a telemetry unit which would allow him to be continually monitored. She assured me that, although he was quite weak, he was on IV antibiotics and his condition had stabilized. I thanked her, gave her our phone number, and told her that I would be calling back in a little while, after Dad had changed rooms.

While I was waiting, Diane and I began to discuss the possibilities.

"You're going to have to fly down."

"Yeah. It certainly looks that way. If I can just hang around here this afternoon, I can get enough work done, that I can miss a few days without too much of a problem."

"Then, if you have to come back, I can go down; or Bill or Edie can. We can keep things covered for a while, but we might have to find some way to have Dad come north. You know, we could add an addition off of the back of the house. If we put in a bedroom, a den and a bathroom, he could be happy out there. He could even smoke, if he kept it to that part of the house."

"It's a great idea, but I don't think that he'll bite. He might be more willing to stay with Bill and Edie than with us. But I can give it a try."

Now that I knew where Dad was, the stress of the last few days was quickly catching up with me. I was relieved, but very tired. After I was able to make contact with Dad again, I just wanted to lie down and take a nap. But before I was able to do anything, the phone rang.

"Hello, Mr. Weinholtz?"

"Yes."

"My name is Dr. Henry Tagore. I am a cardiologist and internist at Central Regional Hospital, and I am the attending physician who is caring for your father. The nursing staff called me at home to let me know that you had managed to locate him, and I thought that I ought to contact you."

"Thank you very much. I appreciate your call. How is he is he doing?

"Well to be very honest with you, it is quite amazing that your father is still alive. By the time he reached the hospital, it could have gone either way. Most people would not have survived that ambulance ride in his condition. He was extraordinarily weak. But we have hydrated him and given him very strong antibiotics. His condition has improved substantially in only a few hours. He has a remarkably strong constitution."

I was struck by the gentle, concerned tone of Dr. Tagore's voice. Over the years, I had encountered the full range of physician attitudes, and I felt immediately thankful that fate had dealt me someone with a kind, sympathetic demeanor.

"Mr. Weinholtz, I don't want to mislead you though. Your

father's condition is still very delicate, and he could take a serious downturn at any time."

"I understand, Doctor Tagore, and I think that it is important for you to know that my father and I have talked this over many times since my mother's death last year. If his condition does drastically worsen, he does not want any sort of heroic measures to sustain his life. He has a living will that stipulates his wishes. He does not want to go on a ventilator."

"How about intubation? Would he be willing to have a feeding tube?"

"No. He's also made that very clear."

"Certainly, I can respect your father's wishes Mr. Weinholtz, but it is very important that I have your statements witnessed by someone other than just ourselves. Would you mind repeating what you have just told me, while I have my wife listen on our other phone?"

"Of course not."

Dr. Tagore's wife got on their other line, and he walked me through a statement of everything that we had just discussed. When we were done, he told me that he thought that it was important that Dad should have a family member with him. I assured Dr. Tagore that I would come to Florida, as soon as possible. Given that it was mid-afternoon, and I desperately needed a good night's sleep, I told him that I thought that I could get there within twenty-four hours. After I hung up, Diane and I checked the US Air flight schedule, and found an 8:30 AM flight from Hartford to Orlando. I called Bill to talk over our options; and we decided that since it would be easier for me to clear my schedule for a week, I should be the one to go. If Dad was going to need support beyond a week, we would figure something out.

On Sunday morning Diane, the kids and I piled into our minivan and made the twenty-minute drive from our house to the airport. I was traveling light, my briefcase and one carry-on bag. They dropped me off right outside of the terminal.

We all hugged good-bye, and I kissed Diane.

"Give us a call when you get there."

"I will. I want to go straight to the hospital to check on Dad. Then I'll catch another taxi to take me to the Marina Inn, so I can check in, pick up Dad's car, and shoot back to the hospital to spend some more time with Dad. I'll call while I'm at the motel. OK?"

"That's fine. Tell Dad that we all love him, and we hope he's better soon."

"Will do."

"And if Bill or Edie can't go next week, I can fly down to take your place. We'll make it work."

"Thanks, Honey. I love you."

"Love you too. Bye."

"Bye."

It was a bright, sunny day. As my plane lifted off the runway I slouched back in my seat and gazed out at the leafless trees covering the brown Connecticut hills. My thoughts drifted back to other long, emergency trips over the last eight years. There had been many, and I wondered how many more might lay in the future.

5

OAT CELL

We were living in Iowa City at the time, and I had just finished teaching my spring semester classes in the University of Iowa's College of Education. The call came late on a Sunday afternoon, when I was outside doing some yard work. Diane answered the phone and soon came running to get me. She was crying in a frightfully pained way.

"Donn! It's Bill. Nancy….Nancy has lung cancer. They're only giving her six weeks to live."

It was the worst news that I had ever been given. I dearly loved Nancy. The thought of her dying was unbearable. In semi-shock, with my world suddenly turned upside down, I took the phone. Bill, sounding terrible himself, repeated the news, then started fielding my questions.

"God, Bill! How is she handling this? There have to be some options. What's being done?"

Bub and Nancy, 1989

"I haven't talked to her yet. I've only talked to Bub, and he said that Nancy doesn't know how bad it is. The doctors told him when he asked, but Nancy only knows that she has cancer. Because she hasn't asked what her chances are, they haven't told her. From what Bub tells me, Nancy only knows that the doctors want to do chemo and radiation, the whole deal; and she wants to go ahead with it."

"Christ, the side-effects will be hell! Have you talked to Mom and Dad yet?"

"No, Nancy doesn't want to worry them, so I'm not going to call. And she wants you to promise not to call either."

As soon as the words were out of Bill's mouth, I knew that I was in trouble. I had always been inclined to plunge ahead with the truth instead of concealing painful information. I couldn't imagine withholding this from Mom and Dad. We talked once or twice a week throughout the year. What was I going to say?

"Oh, everything is great. Diane and the kids are fine, and I'm expecting an article out soon. I can't wait to get to Ocean City in August!"

"Bill, we've got to tell them. I mean…Mom especially. She's got to know. She can be a real help through all of this, and Nancy may only have six more weeks."

"Yeah, I know, but I said that I wouldn't, and I said that I would tell you not to. That's what Nancy wanted!"

"But, Bill, she doesn't know what the doctors are saying. That changes things a lot."

"Donn, don't tell Mom!"

"Maybe...I...I...don't know. Let's cross that bridge when we come to it. Right now, I've got to see Nancy. Do you think that'll be alright?"

"She'd probably like that. She and Bub are going down to the shore for a long weekend. Maybe you could see them down there, but you'd better clear it with them."

"Right. I'll give them a call. Then I'll get back to you, and let you know what I'm doing. Thanks, Bill."

"Love you, Brother."

"I love you, too."

The news was crushing, and the same thoughts kept relentlessly flashing through my head over and over again:

"Not Nancy!...Not now!...Why did you have to keep smoking those damned cigarettes? I begged you to quit. Christ, it's lung cancer! Not Nancy! Not Nancy...."

I fixated on the way Nancy and I, so many times, had teasing arguments about me bringing her cheap cartons of Marlboros from North Carolina. For seven years, she repeatedly asked. I always refused.

"Come on, Donn. Save your dear, sweet sister some money. When you come up to Ocean City, bring me four or five cartons, and I'll pay you back. They're almost twice the price up here."

"Hell no! I'm not going to be your drug runner. Those things will kill you. I don't want that on my conscience. If you come down and visit, then you can buy them yourself."

"You're impossible."

"But at least you know that I care about you!"

Then, the Christmas before we moved from North Carolina, I caved in and bought her a few cartons. I wrapped them up and put a bow on them. She was thrilled.

"Ah! You really do love me."

"It was against my better judgment. I hate to help an addict, but I figured that you're just going to buy them anyway. I did it because I don't know how much longer we'll be in Chapel Hill. This is a one-time deal!"

"That's OK. It's the thought that counts."

That thoughtfulness was haunting me now. I wished that I had never bought the damned things, and I tried to console myself.

"What difference would it have made? She'd have gotten cancer anyway. Christ, not Nancy! Not Nancy!"

I was drowning in my emotions, and I knew that I wouldn't have any peace until I got to see Nancy. But before calling her about visiting, Diane and I needed to get our plans straight. She and Nancy were very close, and this was going to be incredibly difficult for her too. Both teary-eyed, we hugged and sat down to talk.

"Donn, I'd love to go with you, but it is probably going to be too much if all four of us visit. The last thing in the world that they're going to need is four visitors, including a three-year-old motoring all over the place."

"Yeah, you're right; but you're going to have your hands full, if I'm gone for six days. (Four days of driving and two in Ocean City.) How are you going to juggle teaching and taking care of the kids?"

"I don't know. Hansel and Li-Wen... (our baby sitters) ...will have Phil while I'm in school. But helping Dave with his homework and piano; and putting them both down to bed, after getting dinner and doing the dishes; and then trying to grade papers and get ready for the next day will wipe me out. I'll be a wreck when you get back. Maybe you ought to take David with you. He'd be good company in the car, and I'm sure that I can manage Phil on my own."

"It's a heavy trip to lay on a seven-year-old."

"Yeah, but you know he's going to worry about you the whole time that you are gone. And you know how much he loves Nancy. This might be his last chance to see her in any kind of reasonable condition. I'm sure that she and Bub would love to see him, and for that matter Phil too; but we can't all descend on them. The way things have been lately, Phil might come down with an ear infection, and be up crying in the middle of the night. Take Dave. It won't hurt him to miss a few days of school, and I'll feel better if you have him with you. He'll keep you awake at the wheel."

"OK by me. First, let me call, and see if they want us coming at all."

I dialed Nancy and Bub's number. Bub answered the phone. Complicating things a bit was the fact that Nancy and Bub had separated briefly during the previous year. Nancy and I had talked long and often during that period, and she had made it very clear to me that she hoped for the two of them to get back together. They had been reunited for only a few months, but Bub and I hadn't had any real chance to talk about anything since he had returned home. We had always had a good relationship, but this seemed like a hell of a way to break the ice.

Nancy wasn't home, so we spoke frankly.

"How are you holding up, Bub?"

"About as good as can be expected under the circumstances. This really shits, but what can you do?"

"I wish that I knew! How's Nancy?"

"Well, she's really shaken, but she refuses to let herself get down in the dumps. It's kind of amazing. She hasn't even asked the doctor or me just how bad things are. When I was alone with the oncologist, I asked him what the chances are, but Nancy didn't say a word to him about how long she might have. They say that as long as she doesn't ask, they aren't going to tell. It seems strange to me, but that's how she wants to deal with it."

"So, just how bad is it?"

"Bad! The oncologist said this is a 'small cell cancer' called 'oat cell.' It's not operable, because it spreads so fast. The only thing that you can do is try a combination of radiation treatments and chemotherapy, and hope that you can buy some additional time."

"Yeah, but at what cost to Nancy?"

Two friends of mine had each recently given up on chemotherapy because they saw no further hope in that route. Neither was willing to suffer further side effects. Both had cancer of the liver; and both sought relief, maybe even a long-shot cure, through "natural" treatments. One used laetrile, the other high volume doses of juices freshly squeezed from organic vegetables. Neither survived, but both achieved an inspiring peace prior to their deaths. Hospices played vital, supportive roles in each case. Drawing on their experiences and my intuition, I strongly opposed ravaging a body with chemicals unless there was some reasonable expectation of survival. I couldn't set an exact probability for "reasonable," but Nancy's chances sounded terribly slim to me; and the thought of her suffering tortuous side effects was hard to accept. As much as it hurt to think of losing her, I found myself hoping that Nancy would forgo chemotherapy and radiation.

"I don't know, Donn. But its gonna be her call, and she seems to want to fight."

"Of course." I conceded "You're right, Bub. You know, I'd really like to come and visit. Is that OK?"

"It's fine with me."

"How do you think Nancy will feel about it?"

"Well, you know your sister. She'll say, 'Oh, you don't have to do that. I'm doing fine.' But she'd like to see you, and there might not be many other chances. We're going down to Ocean City for the weekend and the first few days of next week. Why don't you come then. Do you want me to pick you up at the airport?"

"No. No. I don't want you to have to do that. I was thinking about driving, and maybe bringing David along. We don't want to crowd you, but he'd be good company on the trip, and it would make things easier on Diane back here."

"Diane and Phil are certainly welcome too."

"Thanks Bub, but for now it will be just us."

"Maybe that's best. Lynn and Scott are probably going to come down, and Bill and Edie may show up too."

"Bub, how about Mom and Dad?"

"Nancy doesn't want to worry them. And she doesn't want your mother to drop everything to come up here to take care of her."

"Bub, they've got to find out sooner or later."

"Yeah, I guess so, but Nancy's mind is made up on this."

The whole notion of protecting people you love from the painful truth continued to trouble me. Years before, I had noticed a poster on a friend's office wall. It showed a direct frontal shot of a surfer emerging into gleam-ing sunlight from the overhanging curl of a dangerously large wave. The accompanying message read: *The best way around a problem is through.* Having been a surfer, the image and message stuck with me. I committed to practicing its wisdom by opting for candor, whenever trapped in tough interpersonal binds. Still, I hedged. It was no time to be a bull in a china shop. So, I relied on the same comment that I had used with Bill.

"Well, I guess that we'll have to cross that bridge when we come to it."

"I guess so. When do you expect to get here?"

"We'll leave the first thing in the morning, and it will take us two full days. So expect us about 7:00 on Friday. Don't hold dinner for us. We'll get something on the way."

"OK. How long do you plan to stay?"

"I think that we ought to leave on Monday morning. David will have to get back to school, and you don't need us hanging around too long."

"That's no problem. You can stay longer. We won't be headed up to Philly until the middle of the week."

"Thanks, Bub; but I've got to get back too. I've got to get ready to teach my summer school classes. Monday will be fine."

"If you say so, but if you change your mind, you're welcome to stay."

"Well, we'll see. Give Nancy a hug for me, and tell her that we'll see her on Friday."

"I'll have her give you a call when she gets home."

"Thanks. I'd really like to talk to her. Take good care of yourself too, Bub. I'm so sorry that you have to go through this."

"It's rotten, but I'll just do what I have to do. It's a lot easier on me than on Nancy. We'll see you soon."

I was immensely relieved. Certain that I was going to be able to visit, I could start preparing to go, rather than sitting around worrying about what was going to happen next. I began packing my stuff for the trip, and Diane packed David's. He was horribly saddened when he heard that Aunt Nancy was very sick, but he was thrilled at the prospect of missing a few days of school and going to Ocean City. Things were humming along. Then, of course, Mom called.

"Hi, Donn. How are things?"

"Hi, Mom. Well, I'm busy running around packing for a trip. I've got several weeks until summer school starts, so David and I are going to take a long weekend to go visit Nancy and Bub in Ocean City."

"David and you. That's nice, but why aren't Diane and Philip going to go too?"

"Diane still has to teach. She can't get away now."

It already seemed ridiculous. I wasn't going to be able to lie to Mom about the reason for the trip. I loved and respected her too much to do that, and I was enormously confident in her ability to handle whatever life served up. Everything came blurting out.

"Mom, I hate to have to tell you this, but the reason I'm going is that Bill called me a few hours ago and told me that Nancy has lung cancer."

"Lung cancer.... Oh, no! **Oh, no!**....When did she find out?"

"Just the other day, I think. You know, I'm not even sure exactly when, but I know that she hasn't called you because she doesn't want to worry you and Dad. She told Bill not to call you, and he passed the word on to me. But I just can't hide it from you. I think you two deserve to know what's happening."

As always, Mom recovered her composure quickly. She appreciated knowing.

"Donn, I'm glad that you told me. I wouldn't want it any other way. But if Nancy is worried about me knowing, I'm not going to call her. It is going to be really hard not to, but I've got to respect that. Now tell me, what's her prognosis?"

"It's not good, Mom. I called Bub and he told me that she has a small cell cancer called 'Oat Cell'. It spreads fast and it's inoperable. Nancy may have only six weeks."

Mom didn't respond. So, I continued.

"Still, they're going to try chemotherapy and radiation. There is a chance that they might help."

"How is she holding up?"

"Pretty well from what I can tell. But she doesn't know how bad the prognosis is. She hasn't asked, and nobody has told her. Everybody is talking around it."

"Well, I am going to have to tell your father. He's going to take this very hard. You know he loves Nancy just as though she is his own daughter."

"Yeah, I know, Mom."

"Donn, please keep us informed about how she's doing. I'll call Nancy just like I always do, and maybe she'll tell me; but if she doesn't, I want to know how things are going. If she doesn't have much time, we'll have to drop things here and head up north."

"Not to worry, Mom. I'll make sure that you know everything. But if Nancy directly tells me not to tell you, I'm going to have to let her know that I already have. God! I hope that she doesn't."

"It will all work out, Donn. It always does."

"Yeah, I think so..."

"Have a safe trip, and I'll talk to you when you get back. I love you, Donn."

"I love you too, Mom. Bye."

Talking to Mom provided a second great sense of relief. She was such a steady, reassuring soul; and our conversation reinforced my conviction that it is better to get everything, no matter how terrible, out on the table, so people can deal with it. Still, the events of the day had taken a severe toll on me. It was approaching sunset, and I was exhausted. We ate supper, and I returned to my packing, only to once again be interrupted by the phone. It was Nancy.

"So, I understand that you are going to drive out to see us!"

"Hi, Nancy. Yeah, David and I are going to come....Nancy, I'm so sorry that you have to go through this..."

"Me too, but don't worry."

She sighed slightly, as though she were trying to convince herself.

"Everything is going to work out OK. Seriously, Donn, there isn't any need for the two of you to drive all the way out here. It's going to be hard on Diane for you not to be around, and David will miss too much school."

"Well, he's really not doing any complaining about that. He's up for it, and Diane will be fine. We've got a lot of support around here. The only reason I might not come would be because it might be too hard for you right now."

"Oh, no. Of course not. I don't start my treatments until the end of next week. They said that I might have to take a few days to recover from the chemo, but I feel fine right now. No, it would be nice to see you, if you really want to drive all of that way."

"I really do."

"OK. So, when will you get here?"

"I'm pretty sure that we can be there by Friday evening, sometime after dinner."

"I'll have something for you."

"No, Nancy. Don't worry about that. We'll have to stop for a rest anyway. And getting David something to eat will keep him happy at the end of a long trip."

"Well, I'll have sandwich makings and maybe coleslaw and potato salad, just in case."

"OK. Sounds good. We'll see you soon. Love you, Nancy."

"Love you, too. Bye."

Although it was natural for Diane and me to say it to each other, in my family "I love you" was not usually a tag line at the end of conversations. Mom, Dad, Nancy, Bill and I generally demonstrated our love by either teasing or showing interest, respect or concern; not by making direct statements of affection. The word "love" wasn't likely to appear, unless something was very seriously amiss. So, even though in our shared crisis I had said "I love you" to both Bill and Mom, I hesitated to say it to Nancy, because I didn't want to pile any alarm on top of a situation that she was downplaying. But confronting the possibility her only having six weeks, I just had to spit it out. Though the words in Nancy's response were appropriate, the tone was strained. Something she didn't want to say, but had to. Upon hanging up, I winced. I wanted so badly to comfort her, but I wasn't sure how to do it.

About 8:30 on Thursday morning, David and I said goodbye to Diane and Phil and we headed east in our Dodge station wagon. I was thankful that it was a beautiful, May morning, and that the weather forecast was great for the next five or six days. That would make things easier. We were looking at about twenty-two hours in the car, and experience had taught me that we were much better off if we didn't have to deal with heavy weather.

While driving along Interstate 80 through Iowa's endless cornfields, I became acutely conscious of the fact that this was an awful lot for David to have to handle. Although his birthday was in a few months, he was still only six years old. He'd never even had a pet die, and here he was going off to see a special aunt, possibly for the last time. Of course, he only knew that she was sick. Maybe he didn't have a clue how sick she really was. Maybe he was thinking about his collection of toy robots. The big issue that he had verbalized that morning regarding the trip was whether or not he could sit in the front seat. He had been firm about the fact that if he had to sit in the back, he didn't want to go. This was a major concession for Diane and me, but since the shoulder strap in the front adjusted to almost his size; we agreed, as long as he would sit on a pillow to ensure that the strap crossed his shoulder correctly. Since I couldn't tell where David's head was regarding our trip, I began probing his thoughts, hoping to prepare him a bit; but feeling tentative myself, having no idea where our talk would lead.

"Dave."

"Yeah, Dad."

"How you doin'?"

"OK, Dad"

"I'm really glad that you're keeping me company. Thanks for coming along."

"You're welcome."

"Dave."
"Yeah."
"Are you happy to be going to Ocean City?"
"Yup."
"Aunt Nancy and Uncle Bub are going to be real happy to see you."
"Can we go in the ocean?"
"It's going to be pretty cold, but we can go in."
"Good. Can we go on the boardwalk?"
"It's still a little early. Not much is going to be open, but we can go up and see what's going on."
"Can we go on the rides?"
"I'm pretty sure that they'll be closed."
"Can we get pizza?"
"Yeah. I'm sure that we can get pizza."
"And a snow cone?"
"Absolutely!"
"Good!"
"David."
"Yeah, Dad."
"Do you understand that Aunt Nancy is very sick."
"Uh huh. What does she have?"
"She has lung cancer, Dave."
"What's lung cancer?"
"It's when something called a tumor starts growing in your lung. That's where you breathe inside your chest."
"Is Aunt Nancy going to die?"
"I hope not, Dave. But she could. It will all depend on how well her medicines work."
"I don't want Aunt Nancy to die."
"Neither do I Dave. Neither do I."
"I don't want Aunt Nancy to die!"
"She may be OK, Dave. Aunt Nancy's been through a whole lot during her life. She was very, very sick when she was a little girl,

and she had to spend a full year in the hospital. People thought that she would die then, but she didn't. And then some doctors thought that she would never walk again, but she did. If anybody can get better from this, it's Aunt Nancy."

"Can we help?"

"Geez, Dave. That's why we're visiting. There's not too much else we can do. We can pray for her every night, when we say your prayers before bed. And we can just be there for her, and let her know that we love her. OK?"

"OK."

"Are you OK?"

"Hmm. Hmm."

"I think you are too. This is a lot for a boy your age to deal with. Whenever you want to talk about it, just say so. OK?"

"OK."

I suspected that I was dealing with my own anxiety more than I was attempting to help David with his. But I did feel better for having broached the topic, and I convinced myself that maybe I had comforted Dave somewhat. We didn't discuss Nancy's illness the rest of the trip east. Instead, we became preoccupied with baseball. As we moved across Illinois, we listened to Harry Carey broadcasting the Cubs game versus the Phillies. That night, at a motel in Richmond, Indiana, we watched a Braves game on cable. The next afternoon, we were able to get the Phillies and Cubs again via Phillies' radio affiliates across Pennsylvania. For a couple of diehard baseball fans, it was a good way to travel.

The weekend in Ocean City was a strange blur of activity. Somehow, Nancy managed to be vivacious and gracious through it all. She sent out very clear vibrations that she was not about to spend much time talking about her illness, but she did share with me the details of how she initially went to her internist because of a deep, severe sore throat. She knew that she was experiencing something unusual, but she was shocked by his quick referral to an oncologist.

Nancy and Jenny (Our last visit together in Ocean City), June 13, 1990

Looking tanned and pretty, with her curly gray hair, which she had only recently stopped setting and dying blonde, Nancy never shed a tear, and only displayed a brief, stern look of annoyance when mentioning getting the bad news. In a glance she could convey, "What a pain in the ass, but we are just going to have to deal with it!"

The first night I got Bub aside to ask him how Nancy was doing. He shook his head in amazement, again saying that he was dumbfounded at how Nancy was dealing with everything. Her attitude seemed to be the less talk the better. By early Saturday, it was clear to me that I might as well just relax and have a good time because Nancy was not about to let this turn into anything more than just another of our visits to Ocean City. About noon, Bill and Edie arrived without their kids. They would only stay into the evening. Lynn and Scott, on the other hand, who showed up soon afterward, would stay until Sunday after dinner.

Throughout much of the weekend, when we were out of Nancy's earshot, the rest of us spent time either consoling ourselves or quizzing each other over whether we had learned anything new. Of course, nobody had because there was nothing new to hear. None of us had been talking to Nancy's doctors, and Nancy sure as hell wasn't sharing anything else. Saturday was a warm, sunny day, which I began with a six-mile run on the boardwalk. After visiting with everyone at the house for several hours, David, Lynn and I headed to the beach, just about a block away. Nancy and Bub had purchased a classic, Ocean City, two-story duplex with big awninged porches, right next door to Mom and Dad's old house. Visiting their neighborhood was indeed "coming home" for me, and the morning's run and the walk to the beach were comforting rituals. In spite of the distressing circumstances of our visit, strolling barefoot down the familiar street brought good memories flooding back. No matter what had brought me to Ocean City, I was glad to be there.

I'D RATHER GO OUT SMILING

Scott & Lynn

At the time, Lynn, an artist, was twenty-seven and living and working in Philadelphia. A free spirit, Lynn was a lot of fun; and as we walked, I was struck by how much she had matured since she had graduated from high school and come to North Carolina for a couple of months to live with Diane and me. That hiatus had been prompted by a battle between her and Nancy over Lynn's desire to move into a Philadelphia apartment with her boyfriend. Diane and I happened to be visiting at the time, and we offered our place as an optional halfway house. Since I had always felt like Lynn and Scott were my younger brother and sister, rather than my niece and nephew, it was not such an unusual offer.

In spite of Lynn's acute 'seventeenness' and a few arguments that Diane and I had over the hours that Lynn should be keeping, I was the overly lenient one, the three of us did pretty well together. Lynn and Diane still talk about an Appalachian Mountain camping trip that the two of them took, along with Diane's friend, Katherine. However, after about five weeks the boyfriend showed up, and Lynn went off to Philly with him.

Over the ensuing decade, that relationship and some others had long since passed the way of so many young infatuations; her relationship with Nancy had healed; and Lynn had become an independent, responsible young woman. With her sprightly sense of humor, she was also great with David. In what was clearly the beginning of a tough phase for us all, I especially appreciated her presence. While the sand and air were warm, the ocean, as usual for late May, was frigid. But that wasn't going to stop David from diving in, and he soon coerced Lynn and me into joining him. We had been body surfing and frolicking around for only a few minutes when I noticed that Bill, fully dressed, was walking across the beach towards the water's edge. Figuring that he wanted to talk to me about something, I left Dave with Lynn and headed to shore. As I drew closer, I saw a look on Bill's face unlike any I had ever received from him. It was the scowl he reserved for his kids when he was really angry with them.

"Oh shit, he's pissed off at me. What's this gonna be about?", I thought as we approached each other.

"What's the matter, Bill?"

"I just got off of the phone with Mom. She told me that she knows about Nancy, and that you told her. What are you trying to prove anyway?" There was no running away from it. I had told Mom, and I hadn't told Bill that I had done it. There really hadn't been a natural opportunity to do so. While traveling east, I hadn't called him up to announce it; and the only chance for us to talk since David and I had left Iowa was while we were all at Nancy's that very day. I sure as hell wasn't going to break it to him then.

I was blindsided by his phone conversation with Mom. The situation was terrible and weird, like Bill and I were about to get into the first serious argument of our lives. I shot back pleadingly from my gut.

"Bill, I had to. Mom called me the same afternoon that you did, and I just couldn't lie to her. I love her too much, and she deserves to know. I know it deep inside me. Nancy may not want it, but Mom needs to know!" Much to my surprise, the steely glare immediately softened, and I breathed a sigh of relief. The worst had passed far more quickly than I imagined it would.

"Well, maybe. Maybe not. There's no use arguing about it now. Mom says that she wants us to keep her posted, and that if things take a serious turn for the worse, she and Dad are coming up."

"Good. She's got to be here if that's the case. They're too close for her not to be here."

"Yeah, well when the time comes, you can tell Nancy how Mom found out."

"Fair enough. I guess that goes with the turf."

The rest of the weekend was pleasant and uneventful. While Nancy and Bub stayed close to the house, the rest of us did the sorts of things we would normally do. That night Lynn, Scott and I took David on the boardwalk, and got him his pizza and snow cone. I hadn't gone out with both Lynn and Scott in ages, not since they had both visited us for a week in North Carolina, when they were about twelve and fourteen. Unlike Lynn, Scott had continued living at home, learning the tree trimming business while working for Asplundh, a large tree care company. Eventually, with Nancy's support, he started his own successful business, Scott's Tree Service. Always a congenial guy, Scott had developed into an exceptionally hardworking and reliable person. He was also extraordinarily devoted to his mother.

As much as I enjoyed myself as we walked along, I ached over the fact that I wouldn't be around more to provide both Lynn and Scott with more support as Nancy's cancer progressed. And I was feeling especially bad about Scott. Prior to me going off to college and getting married, he had been like my little brother. But I had seen precious little of Scott since Diane and I had moved to Galveston, and then to Iowa. I didn't say anything about it, but I was feeling like I had abandoned everyone by moving so far away. I suddenly recognized the extreme distance, previously only a nagging irritant, would no longer be tolerable.

Sunday was another good beach day. Then on Monday, Dave and I headed back to Iowa. The good-byes were hard, but not as traumatic as I had expected.

Nancy was too upbeat, and the trip had diffused my shock and terror, leaving only the profound sadness at living so far away. As we drove west, my concerns about the distance were underscored by the weather conditions. On Monday evening, we encountered a treacherous storm front just east of Cleveland. Things got so bad that I exited Interstate 80 earlier than I had intended, and we checked into a motel. When we turned on the TV to watch the weather report, the weather map showed tornadoes all around us. I figured that they would pass through and that we would have clear sailing on Tuesday, but there was no such luck. A big stationary trough stretched all the way to Chicago, and we bumped into one violent storm after another. I detested the drive more than ever.

The next month, we returned to Ocean City. The week before Nancy's fiftieth birthday, Diane's ninety-eight year old grandmother, Ella JaneSmith, died. Following her husband Gary's death in 1967, Grandmother Smith lived by herself for nearly twenty years in their Carney's Point, New Jersey cottage. When her occasional falls began occurring too frequently, she moved to a nursing care facility close to Diane's parents. She remained extraordinarily sharp until very near the end of her life, and she was beloved and respected by all. Naturally, everyone in Diane's family, including all of us, made the trek to the Eastern Shore of Maryland, site of the historic family cemetery, for the funeral.

This left us only a short ferry ride across the Delaware Bay from the South Jersey shore. Since Bub was planning a surprise birthday party for Nancy we decided to pop over, and join the fun. When we arrived, we discovered that there was an even bigger surprise. Unknown to Nancy, Mom and Dad, who had driven up from Florida, were due to arrive within minutes.

Once again, Nancy, now wearing a wig following her chemotherapy, was the life of the party; greeting everyone, joking about everything, and telling us all that we didn't have to bring her presents. She seemed deeply touched by our family making it to the party, but she was flat-out stunned when Mom made her appearance. Looking great for a seventy-six year old woman in frail health, Mom—ramrod straight, tastefully dressed, and sporting a stylish wig of her own—flowed into the party and headed straight over to Nancy, who was sitting at a large circular table on the front porch. Mom's characteristic smile radiated pleasure, comfort and control. She was not about to let this get messy.

I couldn't make out what Mom whispered to Nancy as Nancy stood to give her a hug, but there was a moment of hush, a few tears on each of their parts, and then relieved laughter, causing everyone else to join in. Everything seemed fine. The synchrony between the two was startling. Though cancer was in our midst, the world appeared in order; at least for awhile.

An hour or so later, I was standing in the kitchen pouring a drink, and Nancy walked in. At that moment, Bub was the only other person there and, out of the blue, Nancy casually asked me if I had talked to her general internist, Dr. Fitzpatrick. During David's and my trip to Ocean City, Nancy had suggested that I give him a call, because he could fill me in much better than her on what was occurring with her cancer. I had called him and told him what I already knew. He, in turn, was quite open with me, saying that he was especially fond of Nancy and that he was saddened because her prospects were poor.

"The problem is that Oat Cell spreads so quickly. By the time you discover it, there is no hope of surgically removing it. The only thing that you can do is rely on combinations of chemotherapy and radiation to slow its development. You keep changing the drugs because the disease rapidly develops resistance to them, but then eventually you run out of drugs."

"I was told that she might only have six weeks," I responded to Dr. Fitzpatrick.

"That's sometimes the case, but quite often additional time can be bought. It varies from individual to individual, depending on how early you discover the cancer, how well the patient tolerates the treatments, and the patient's will and determination to live. In that regard, the way that Nancy overcame her polio has already shown that she has a remarkable survival instinct. But I'll be honest with you, her chances are very slim. Still, I've learned that there are people out there who can beat the very worst odds. Hopefully, she'll be one of them."

I was taken aback by the way that Nancy slipped me the question about Dr. Fitzpatrick, and I offered an indirect response.

"Yeah. I gave him a call. He seemed like a really good guy."

"He is. What did he have to say?"

She hit me right between the eyes with that one. Her head was tilted a bit, and she had a curious look on her face. After weeks of public denial, Nancy had decided to go fishing for the truth, and she had chosen to come to me.

I thought, "Jesus Christ, why now? What am I going to do? I had grown used to the fact that Nancy wasn't going to talk about her condition. I never expected this. Cornered, my plunge ahead with the truth reflexes took over.

"Well Nancy. It's a serious cancer, and the chances aren't great;

but he told me that the results can differ amazingly from patient to patient. If you really rise to the challenge, you might be able to beat this."

It was out! I had spilled the beans, and the immediate results weren't encouraging. Nancy stayed composed, but a deeply unsettled look shot across her face. I could see that she was struggling not to lose it. Moving to the counter, she poured herself an iced tea.

"I guess that's just what I'm going to have to do."

"If anybody can, it's you Nancy. That's one of the things that he told me. You've got a great attitude for fighting this."

"I hope so. I suppose that we'll see. Thanks. I've got to get back and visit."

Nancy turned, and headed out to the porch, while some of the guests filed into the kitchen. I was dazed by the rapid turn of events, and I had never in my life been so unsure of my actions. The power of the truth seemed awfully weak at the time. I walked around the house for a while, and eventually bumped into Nancy again, who on the surface seemed fully recovered. She asked me if I could go downstairs to the back of the house, and transfer a load of towels, that had been sitting unattended for hours, from the washer to the dryer. I said, "Sure," and I headed down. I was in the midst of loading the dryer, when I noticed that Bub had followed me. Drink in hand, he was standing behind me, visibly angry.

"Just what in the hell were you trying to do? Who do you think you are telling her she's going to die?"

I was deeply shaken. Although still strongly in favor of frankly discussing things with Nancy, I had never intended for us to have the kind of in-passing conversation that we had just shared. Now, on top of feeling badly, I was going to have to deal with the peripheral fallout. Fighting back tears, I shot back.

"Bub, I'm really sorry. Nancy caught me completely by surprise. She asked me point blank, and I felt that I had to tell her what Fitzpatrick said. But I didn't tell her that she was going to die. I told her that the odds aren't great, but that she may be able to beat this."

"Yeah, well that's not the way it sounded to me!"

"Bub, please believe me. I didn't want to have that conversation with Nancy. At least not like that. I feel terrible. I know that this is much worse on her and on you, and I'm just blowing in from out of town; but I love Nancy so much. Shit, this is killing me too. I don't want to do anything to hurt either of you."

Then I began to cry, and seeing me falling apart caused Bub to soften appreciably.

"I know you wouldn't. It...it was just hard for me to hear. Nancy won't even talk about it with me. Then all of a sudden, she's asking you."

I started to get a grip on myself.

"I guess that this stuff has to start coming out somehow, but this isn't at all like I expected. For some reason she really needs to keep it in. But she wouldn't have asked me what she did, if she didn't need to talk about it."

"So tell me. What did Fitzpatrick say?"

"Pretty much what I said upstairs. The odds are never good in Nancy's situation, but there is a chance. He was emphatic about the fact that you can't tell in advance how someone is going to respond to treatment."

"That's not the way the cancer specialist gave it to me."

"I know, but Fitzpatrick feels that she might do quite a bit better than six weeks; and there is always the remote chance that she could beat it altogether."

"That's the first positive news that I've gotten at all."

"I guess what's positive is all relative, but there is a glimmer of hope."

"Yeah, but a glimmer is better than nothing."

Bub and I talked a little longer, gave each other a brief hug, then headed back upstairs to the party. I felt quite a bit better than

I had; but I was still tense, and haunted by uncharacteristic self-doubts.

"Who am I to break everything wide open? How can I help here when I'm off living in Iowa? Jesus, how stupid can I get?"

These questions nagged at me the rest of the day and throughout the drive back to Iowa City. By the time we got home, I had made up my mind that I was going to look for a job back east. We had too many relatives in the northeast, and living almost a thousand miles away was now simply unbearable. Our parents and aunts and uncles were getting old; and as Nancy had taught us, our generation was growing vulnerable. I decided that I wouldn't sell my soul for just any job. It would have to be something I would be comfortable with, but I vowed that I wouldn't stop searching until we had gotten substantially closer to home.

6

AT BOTH ENDS

Sometime after 5:00 p.m., I arrived home from work and rushed into the house to gather our bags. Diane and I wanted to pack the car and hit the road before too late. If we hurried, the April daylight would hold up long enough for us to cross the mountains between Johnson City, Tennessee, where we had moved the previous summer, and Boone, North Carolina. Then, with the worst of the winding roads behind us, we could stop for a leisurely supper, continuing on to Chapel Hill after dark. We were eagerly anticipating the trip, as it had been ten years since our 1980 departure from Chapel Hill. I had only been back once, to defend my doctoral dissertation in 1981; and Diane hadn't been back at all. So, I quickly accepted when I received an invitation to give a presentation on my research findings at a conference hosted by the University of North Carolina School of Medicine. We could make a long weekend of it, leaving on Wednesday and returning on Sunday. Better yet, Diane's parents could come and stay with Dave and Phil, so they wouldn't miss any school; while Jenny, our twenty-two-month old, born before we left Iowa, could accompany us. The three of us would fit snugly in a small room at the Carolina Inn on the UNC campus, where Diane and I stayed when we first visited Chapel Hill in 1973.

I was frantically running around trying to pull things together for the trip; while also attending to the boys, whose feelings were bruised because they weren't going along. In the background, I heard the telephone ring; and I was pleased when Diane's mother picked it up, because I didn't want to be bothered. But when she called out to me saying that Aunt Mary was on the other end, I knew immediately that something had to be seriously wrong, because in my entire life Aunt Mary had never telephoned me about anything.

I dashed for the phone, and cut quickly through the niceties.

"Hi, Aunt Mary. What's up?"

"Bad news, Donn. Your mother had to go to the hospital in Port St.Lucie. The doctors say that her lungs have a lot of fluid in them, and her condition doesn't sound very good."

Even though Mom's internist, Dr. Johnstone, had recently called and alerted me to the fact that Mom's diabetes, heart disease and associated kidney problems made her "frail," I was caught by surprise. During the previous twenty years, Mom had overcome a heart attack and breast cancer without slowing down too greatly. So when Dr. Johnstone said "frail," I understood him to mean that there might be problems a few years down the line. I never expected anything within the month. Still, Mom had been bothered by a nagging cough since Christmas, and I had warned her it might be due to a micoplasma infection, the cause of so-called "walking pneumonia." In mid-March I suggested that she see Dr. Johnstone and request a ten-day course of erythromycin. She did, and soon after she began taking the medicine, the cough subsided. However, it returned a few days after her prescription was completed, and I then urgently insisted that Mom request a second round of erythromycin. She assured me that she would, so I assumed that everything would be fine. Eventually, I found out that when Mom called Dr. Johnstone, he was on vacation. When confronted with another physician, instead of insisting on more erythromycin, Mom settled for a cough medicine. Her cough soon flared into pneumonia, and then into congestive heart failure.

My head was spinning as I was trying to figure out what to do. Then Aunt Mary dropped the second bomb.

"It gets worse, Donn. Nancy has been readmitted to the hospital in Philadelphia. Her lung cancer has reappeared and the doctors are suggesting surgery."

This was the real punch to the stomach. For almost three years, Nancy had startled her physicians and everyone else by responding remarkably well to her chemotherapy and radiation treatments. Then to our overwhelming joy, following an exhaustive regimen of tests, at Christmas she had been declared "clean" of cancer. It appeared that Nancy's indomitable will had once again overcome the greatest of challenges. But now she was facing "surgery." By that time, I knew enough about oat cell to know that this could only be a last ditch effort to extend Nancy's life a bit longer. I wondered how this devastating reversal could have come so fast. Nancy's aura of invincibility had grown even stronger with each of her several remissions. If anyone was going to beat the prognosis, it was her. But now the doctors were resorting to surgery. After three years of holding out for a miracle, I suddenly lost all hope of a cure. Standing there in Tennessee, I felt cruelly torn, wanting to be with both Mom and Nancy, but not having a clue about what to do. Physically shaking, I thanked Aunt Mary for calling, and indicated that I planned to phone each in their respective hospital rooms. Then came a familiar and frustrating hitch.

"By the way, neither one wants the other to know that she is in the hospital."

"OK, Aunt Mary. I won't tell either for now. We'll give this some time and see what happens."

In spite of my previous inclinations towards brutal honesty, I did intend to hold my tongue. Living with Nancy's disease for so long, after her initial "six-week" prognosis, had taught me that the urgency of the moment could be misleading. I knew that we would eventually have to come clean, but it seemed best to remain patient for the moment. So, when I called Nancy, and listened to her cheerfully tell me not to worry, I agreed to her request "not to tell Mom." Then when I called Mom, who spoke haltingly and wasn't convincing at all in her efforts to put a positive spin on things, I promised her not to call Nancy; knowing all the while, it would be nearly impossible to play along as these two, who loved each other so much, kept each other in the dark.

Trying to show some of Mom's hard-headed pragmatism, I sized up the situation, and decided not to go jetting off to either place. Nancy was not in any immediate danger and had plenty of support in Philadelphia; and it wasn't yet clear if Mom's condition warranted a visit. I was obligated to give my presentation, on teaching by attending physicians, at 2:00 p.m. the next day. So, after quickly touching base with Bill, Lynn, and Dad; I decided to push on to Chapel Hill, monitoring both situations by telephone and doing whatever seemed required as events dictated. Unfortunately, by the time all the phone calls were completed, it was already dark outside. I was inclined to hit the road anyway, but Diane argued convincingly that we should get a good night's sleep and leave early the next day. Feeling emotionally drained, I agreed.

By morning, the previous day's sunshine gave way to dark gray clouds and pouring rain; mountain weather at its dreariest. We departed about 7:00 A.M., heading east towards Chapel Hill. Diane and I have always enjoyed our time together in the car because of the uninterrupted opportunity for talk, and we tried to remain upbeat. However, the weather and the circumstances threw a wet blanket over everything. We cracked lame jokes, but kept returning to the fact that we were both deeply worried about Mom and Nancy; and as the rain came down in sheets, we were also concerned about whether or not we would get through the mountains alive.

The trip took over an hour longer than it normally would, but we pulled safely into the driveway of the Carolina Inn at approximately noon. To our pleasant surprise, Vance Riggsbee, one of Diane's students from Chapel Hill High School, was a bellman at the Inn. His warm greeting and the beautiful UNC campus brought back a flood of pleasant memories. The weather was still drab, but the prospects for the visit seemed a little brighter.

After checking in, we grabbed a bite to eat at the Inn's dining room. Then Diane, taking Jenny in a stroller, went to knock around town, while I went over to the auditorium where I was scheduled to give my presentation. Although preoccupied with Nancy's and Mom's health while crossing the campus, I was able to become totally absorbed in the two-hour interactive session that followed. Having researched attending physician teaching for over ten years, I was in the middle of completing a book closing my work on the topic and was as primed for the session as possible. It went very well and was therapeutic. Also, when it was over there was the relief of knowing that my primary obligation was fulfilled, freeing us to leave at any time.

Diane, Jenny and I met up about 5:00 p.m. and strolled around campus a bit before heading to The Rathskeller, an old student and faculty haunt, for dinner. The rain gave way to a damp mist; and as we walked through the tree-lined, academic quadrangles with their 19th century, Georgian buildings, we talked obsessively about Nancy and Mom. The surroundings were strangely soothing, helping us to schizophrenically juxtapose our current worries with fond recollections.

After dinner, we returned to our room to shower before attending a reception held in conjunction with the conference.

One of Diane's former students was going to watch Jenny. It would be good to have the time for just the two of us; but before going out, we wanted to call and check on both Nancy and Mom to let them know that we had arrived safely and to see how things were going. We chatted briefly with Nancy. She seemed pretty good, and had nothing new to report.

Mom, on the other hand, had taken a turn for the worse. Her speech was halting and slurred, completely out of character for her; and she sounded absolutely exhausted. First, she told me how her physicians had drained a large volume of fluid from her lungs, and how they were amazed that she hadn't complained a bit about the pain. She prided herself on her stoicism and was trying to show me that she was still in control; but her voice just didn't match the image she wanted to convey. Next, she tried to comfort me saying, "They assure me that it's very unlikely that I have cancer."

Since cancer hadn't occurred to me as a possible diagnosis, this was not a pick-me-up; but I told her that it was good news and that I loved her very much. Then I asked to speak to Dad, who was at her bedside.

Dad was shell-shocked. He told me that Mom was "not in real good shape," but that at least she wasn't desperately gasping for air and "seeing elephants" (hallucinating due to hypoxia) like she was when he first brought her in at 3:00 a.m. the day before. I asked if I should fly down. He told me that he didn't think so because Mom was getting good care, and there probably wasn't anything for me to do. I agreed with him, assured him that I would come immediately, if necessary, then hung up. We went on to the reception, a real up-scale event held in the nearby Research Triangle Park, but the entire time we were there, I fixated on Mom's condition. Afterwards, I slept very poorly; and when morning finally rolled around, got up early and went running. Finally, the sun was shining brightly, and the Chapel Hill scenery, assisted by a healthy dose of endorphins, soothed my rattled nerves. Returning to our room feeling more upbeat, I showered and stayed with Jenny while Diane went on a run of her own. After Diane showered, we headed off to Breuger's Bagels for a quick breakfast, and we made plans to meet for lunch following a morning session on curriculum reform that I wanted to attend.

Upon arriving at the session, all of the seats were taken except for a few in the first row, where I parked myself; serendipitously sitting next to Bill Mattern, one of the presenters and the Associate Dean for AcademicAffairs at the UNC School of Medicine. Bill was the person who had gained me entree to UNC'S Department of Internal Medicine for my dissertation research. After I completed the study, we collaborated with Chuck Friedman, my dissertation advisor, on an article summarizing the research for the *New England Journal of Medicine*. It was good to see Bill, and I was looking forward to hearing what he had been up to over the last several years.

I never got the chance. Early in the session, Jamie Shumway, a friend from graduate school who had become an associate dean at West Virginia University's medical school, tapped me on the shoulder and whispered in my ear:

"Donn, Diane is in the back of the auditorium. Your mother has taken a turn for the worse. It looks like you should go to Florida."

Taken by surprise, I mumbled some sort of apology to Bill, and followed Jamie back to Diane who was standing in the lobby with Jenny strapped in her stroller. Diane looked terribly worried, and as the four of us moved outside, she filled me in on the details. Mom's attending physician, Dr. Patel, had called our room and caught Diane just as she was stopping by to drop off some items that she had purchased. He told her that Mom's lungs were again filling with fluid, her kidneys were failing, and they were likely going to have to put her on a respirator. He indicated that "the end" might come soon, and that it would be wise for me to fly down to Florida as soon as possible.

We thanked Jamie for his help, and headed downtown to a travel agency to book plane tickets. On the way, we decided that it would be best if I went alone with Diane and Jenny returning by car to Johnson City. I got booked on an afternoon flight out of Raleigh-Durham Airport. Then, having several hours to kill, we stopped by Carolina Book and Supply, where I bought a copy of Clyde Edgerton's *The Floatplane Notebooks* to read on the flight. Though usually preferring non-fiction, for once I desperately wanted to lose myself in a good novel. Diane and I had taught with Clyde's wife, Susan, at Chapel Hill High School; and I had talked with Clyde several times when we were both in grad school at UNC, well before he was being touted in some circles as "the next Faulkner." I hadn't read any of his other books, but I hoped that he might provide the catharsis of a world completely different from my own.

Our last stop was the Carolina Coffee Shop, another old favorite spot featuring soft classical music and a cozy, den-like atmosphere. We tried to enjoy a meal, but we were both too numb. With Mom's death appearing imminent, it was especially tough knowing that Nancy couldn't be with her. Hope, a constant companion over the previous three years, was nowhere in sight.

While driving to the airport, we nailed down our strategy. Bill and Edie had already flown to Florida from Philadelphia. They would meet me at the West Palm Beach airport and drive us to the hospital. After returning to Johnson City, Diane would assess how well the kids could handle staying with her parents; and if everything seemed alright, she would fly down as soon as possible. All the while, I was hating the thought of separating, knowing that I would worry about Diane and Jenny until I knew that they were safely back in Tennessee.

The US Air terminal came all too soon, and there was no need for Diane and Jenny to park and see me off. It would only delay their departure for Tennessee. So, I kissed them both good-bye, pulled my bag and briefcase from the back of our minivan, and waved to them as they drove away. Soon, I was on the plane, where I found myself drifting back and forth between my own worries and those of the Copelands of Listre, North Carolina, the family straight out Clyde's imagination. The book helped a lot, and I clung to it over the next several days, reading just enough to distract me, but not so much that I would finish it too soon.

Edie, Bill and I drove by Mom and Dad's condo in Vista del Lago; then continued up U.S. Route 1 to the HCA (Hospital Corporation of America) Hospital of Port St. Lucie. When we arrived, things weren't good. Mom, who was in intensive care, was increasingly hypoxic and fluttering back and forth between hallucinations and brief lucid moments. It was difficult to have any sort of conversation with her; and within two days, after a convincing sell from Dr. Patel, we agreed to placing Mom on a respirator, in the hope of reversing the downward spiral of her heart and kidney functions. It was to be a short-term intervention. If positive results were not quickly forthcoming, we all agreed to take Mom off of the respirator, to allow her to die.

Although he signed the necessary papers to prevent any further heroic measures if we removed Mom from the respirator, Dad could barely bring himself to talk about what was happening. Mom was only allowed two visitors at a time, for a 15-minute period each hour. When Dad couldn't be by Mom's side, he sat mournfully watching TV in the waiting room. He only opened up when we left the hospital for lunch or dinner. Then, with the help of a few Manhattans, his anguish poured out.

"Why me? First my father, then my mother and now Gada! Why do I have to bury everyone that I ever loved?"

It was as though all the years between my grandparents' deaths and Mom's current crisis were condensed to just a few, with the many good times in between dwarfed by the pain of death's searing moments. Most often, we would just listen, put our arms around Dad's shoulders, and acknowledge how much we too loved Mom and him. But with things going the way they were, we soon had to let him know why Nancy wasn't flying down; a discussion that only deepened his sorrow and our own. Still, we somehow found opportunities to joke about how tough-minded Mom would want us to deal with everything. Those moments, again assisted by the Manhattans, helped a bit. And at one point, I told Dad how most people would be envious of the forty-plus years that he had spent with Mom. Tears in his eyes, he acknowledged his good fortune.

Throughout, we couldn't have asked for a more humane physician than Dr. Patel. While carefully explaining the relationships among the deterioration of heart, lung and kidney functions, he gently acknowledged Mom's tremendous will to live.

"Though rare, I have seen cases where strong-minded patients have rallied and conquered conditions as serious as your mother's. Her chances of survival are remote, but not impossible. She is a remarkable woman, and she could surprise us all."

Still, he assured us that he would not battle with us, if Mom's condition worsened, and we felt that it was time to let her slip away. He was our ally in the cause, no matter what the outcome.

Over the next few days, we became obsessed with Mom's laboratory results, particularly focusing on her kidney functions, as a critical side effect of congestive heart failure is kidney shutdown. We hung on each set of lab tests, hoping against the odds for dramatic improvement. Instead, in spite of a few teasing stable counts, the overall trends dropped steadily downward. Meanwhile, I spent an inordinate amount of time on the phone explaining the lab numbers of the moment to relatives around the country, all of whom wanted to be kept abreast of events. I complemented myself on holding together so well, but began feeling increasingly drained. Stress was taking its toll.

Edie and Bill, 1991

The most stressful thing of all was telling Nancy, who only knew that Bill and Edie were in Florida visiting Mom and Dad. Mom's condition had deteriorated to the point that we all felt that she had to know the truth. After talking it over with Bill, Edie and Dad, I called Nancy in her hospital room.

"Hi! How are you doing?"

"Oh, hi, Donn. Pretty good, but I've got a bad cold now, and they have to postpone the surgery until I get rid of it."

"Is that good news or bad?"

"Well, I don't know. I wasn't exactly looking forward to getting cut open; but on the other hand, it would be good to just get it out of the way." "Yeah, well maybe its best that you not have the surgery for a little while. Nancy, I'm calling from Florida. Mom was taken to the hospital with congestive heart failure. She didn't want to worry you, so she told us not to call. But she has gotten so much worse that we had to put her on a respirator. Things don't look good, and if she continues to deteriorate, we're going to have to take her off and let her go."

"Oh, no! No! No! No!"

"I'm so sorry, Nancy. I wish that I didn't have to tell you this."

"Is there any chance that she might make it?"

"There's a small chance. She's really tough, and she's not giving up; but her numbers are headed in the wrong direction. She can't breathe on her own, and her kidneys aren't doing well at all."

Though she was willing to die, I was newly aware of Mom's determination to live. Earlier in the day, we had been alone together. I was holding her hand, and asked her if she wanted to come off of the respirator even if it meant dying. Looking tired, but clear-eyed, unable to speak because of the respirator, she nodded yes. Then I asked how she felt about dying. Painfully, slowly, with words nearly sloping off the page of a notepad we had given her, she scratched out her answer.

"I'm not afraid, but it's hard to die when there is so much to live for."

We stared, through our tears, into each other's eyes. I squeezed her hand and told her how much I loved her, and how nobody had ever had a better mother. I felt a deep sense of loss knowing that my dear friend's time was nearly up, along with the bittersweet good fortune of telling Mom just how much she meant to me.

That's what was making this call to Nancy so difficult. I wanted her to have the same chance.

"I want to come right now. But I can't while I'm this sick. They wouldn't even let me in to see her. This is awful. Listen, tell Mom that I love her; but that I've just got to get better before I can fly down. Tell her that I'll be there as soon as I can. Tell her that I'll make it by sometime next week."

"OK, Nancy. I will."

"And call me every day to let me know what is happening."

"OK, Nancy. Love you."

"I love you too."

I could hear that Nancy was fighting back tears. It ripped me up because there was so little chance that Mom was going to live beyond a few days, and Nancy probably wouldn't be able to make it to Florida in time to say goodbye. Events the next day confirmed my worst suspicions. Dr. Patel saw us about noon, and reported that Mom's test results were continuing to cascade downward. She was unconscious most of the time. The respirator was keeping her alive, but it wasn't having the desired effect of triggering a recovery. The time had come. We asked Dr. Patel to remove Mom from the respirator. He assured us that he would comply with our wishes; but suggested that we allow her one more night. We agreed, and after staying until around 8:30 PM, left for a late and somber supper. We steeled ourselves for a hard day as we drove to the hospital the next morning, knowing that Mom would not die immediately after coming off of the respirator, but not knowing what else to expect. What we least expected was the news that we received.

While walking toward the intensive care unit, we were greeted by a smiling Dr. Patel. He addressed Dad.

"I have very good news. As I said before, your wife is indeed a remarkable woman. When we removed her from the respirator this morning, she immediately began breathing on her own. She is receiving supplemental oxygen, but she appears to have stabilized. She is not out of the woods yet. She is still in very serious condition, but this is a very favorable sign."

Another reprieve! Somehow having dodged a bullet, we clung

to new hope, particularly buoyed by the fact that, now off of the respirator, Mom could once again talk.

Dad and I went in to visit first. Mom's eyes immediately locked on to Dad's, and she blurted out, "Hello, Bill. I love you;" and the two of them chatted away, while I stood there like a piece of furniture.

"I love you too. You had me a little scared there. I wasn't sure you were going to make it off of that machine alright."

"Well, I don't want all of those widows at Vista bringing you casseroles yet."

"You don't have to worry about that. There will never be anyone but you."

"No, someday you can set up house with someone else. Just not yet."

"Whatever you say, Dear."

I took it as a positive sign that it didn't take long before they bickered a little over how Mom should dispose of her tissues. Mom was showing her spunk.

"Gada, now just reach over here and drop your tissue in the trash can on the floor. It's so easy and you don't have to look at the dirty tissues on your bed."

"I prefer that pink, plastic tub over there. Give it to me. If I put it here next to me in bed, it's so much easier."

"But the other way is easy, and you don't have to look at all of those lousy tissues. This way is best, after all it was suggested by an engineer." Pulling professional rank didn't work.

"Look, this is how a housewife does it. I wipe my mouth, and I flick it in the tub. See how easy it is."

"Okay, case closed. You win."

After a little while, Dad said that he would go get Bill and Edie, so they could have a chance to visit too. I waited behind so I could have my own opportunity to talk to Mom. As Dad went out the door, she chirped, "Good-bye, Bill. You're the best husband I've ever had."

As soon as Dad disappeared around the corner, Mom turned and looked me squarely in the eye. Her tone became serious. She wanted to deal with immediate business.

"Now, here's the thing, Donn. If I take a turn for the worse, I don't want that tube going down my throat again, and I don't want anyone thumping on my chest trying to revive me. After all, why prolong things! And what do you call it after you die, and they cut you up to find out what happened to you?"

"An autopsy."

"Autopsy, yes. Absolutely no autopsy!"

"Okay, Mom. Don't worry. I'll take care of everything."

I had my marching orders. No more respirator! No more heroic measures!

Throughout, I had been speaking with Diane several times a day. We quickly decided that she would not fly to Florida because the kids were very upset at the prospect of her leaving. Then, once Mom took a turn for the better, we made plans for me to fly back to Tennessee so we could all return to Florida by car. I would take a week's vacation. Diane, who was involved in a National Science Foundation grant working with teachers in rural schools, and the kids would all have off because of spring break. Edie and Bill, who had already tapped heavily into their vacations, would stay in Florida until the day that we were scheduled to return. Diane and I could stay for the week, but then we would have to head home, as I couldn't afford to miss any more work. After our departure, it would be completely up in the air as to who would might stay with Mom and Dad. We all desperately hoped that Nancy would recuperate quickly from her cold, and be sufficiently strong to visit.

Her first few days off of the respirator, Mom did pretty well. So, I headed back to Tennessee, cleared up a few items at work, gathered the family, and made the sixteen hour drive back to Florida. Unfortunately, by the time we returned, Mom's kidneys were failing. One was not functioning at all. The other was in steady decline, and she was displaying the characteristic sluggishness of uremic poisoning, talking slowly and regularly drifting off to sleep. Unexpectedly, Diane and I found ourselves confronted by a new dilemma, whether or not to urge Mom to undergo acute dialysis in an effort to revive her steadily deteriorating kidney.

By then, Mom's cardiologist, Dr. Johnstone, back from vacation, was sharing Mom's case with Dr. Patel, one of his practice partners. This was a psychological boost for Mom, because she greatly respected and trusted Johnstone. He, too, was sensitive to our family's requests for no further heroic measures, and neither physician applied any pressure regarding attempting dialysis. On the contrary, they gently warned us that if Mom agreed to dialysis, they would then have to defer to the nephrologists, who would take over primary responsibility for Mom's case. Since Dad had delegated all medical strategizing to us, Diane and I found ourselves struggling over what to do. One evening we went walking on the macadam paths encircling the lakes at Vista del Lago. I was particularly tormented.

"Diane, she's already been through so much. Dialysis is supposed to be incredibly demanding, and she's told me that she doesn't want the respirator again. I can't ask her to do this just for us."

"I know what you mean, but she still has that spark. Even though she is sleeping so much, she's so sharp when she's awake. The nephrologists think that they might be able to pull her out of this."

"That's what they're trained to think. Even when the odds are way against them, they see some way of pulling things out. And lot's of times doctors become aggressive to avoid malpractice charges. If we talk her into signing on with another team of doctors, there is no telling how far they are going to push. After all, Johnstone and Patel aren't really advocating this."

"No, they aren't. But given the way Mom seems, can you really let her go now without giving it a shot?"

Diane's last question nailed me to the wall. In spite of all of my realist talk about letting go, I wasn't prepared to do so while Mom, though on death's door, was still lucid and had a remote chance of surviving.

"No, I can't. But we're going to have to make sure that there's some way to get out of this, if Mom doesn't improve."

So, we decided to talk to Dad and to Mom about giving acute dialysis a try. As expected, Dad's response was, "Whatever you think is best."Mom, on the other hand, wasn't immediately convinced. In her increasingly slurred speech, she made it clear that she was still in charge.

"Donn, I want some time to think about it. Give me tonight. I appreciate that you all want to keep me around, but I've got to be sure that I want to keep on going like this."

"Okay, Mom. I understand. I love you, but I'm prepared if you have to let go. Let's see how you feel in the morning."

The next day, before going to see Mom, Diane, Dad and I dropped by Dr. Johnstone's and Dr. Patel's office in order to alert them that we were expecting a decision from Mom about whether or not to proceed with dialysis. The night before, I had given Mom's health update to relatives all over the east coast; and once again, I found the ongoing reporting particularly taxing, especially when talking to Nancy, who was showing no signs of being sufficiently well to make the trip from Philadelphia. But we were all wearing down, so I thought nothing of it when Dad asked if he and Diane could sit outside together, while I went in to talk to the two physicians. I understood completely that he couldn't handle discussing the consequences if Mom refused dialysis.

After checking in with the receptionist, I was pleasantly surprised at being immediately escorted into the doctors' shared office. Dr. Johnstone and Dr. Patel were sitting at separate desks, both facing me, their backs to a large window, revealing palm trees and the hospital in the background. We shook hands, and I pulled up a seat about ten feet in front of their desks. After explaining to them my conversation with Mom about dialysis, and telling them this would be the morning of her decision, I reminded them that, should Mom decide against dialysis, she and our family didn't want any further heroic measures. They nodded their understanding. Then, I went on to the topic of what might happen if Mom selected dialysis, but continued on a downward course, requesting their help in then being able to discontinue the dialysis. At which point, they reiterated what they had previously told me, that their hands would be tied, as the nephrologists would be in primary control. While it was not what I wanted to hear, I took solace in the fact that the one nephrologists whom I had met, Dr. Rodriguez, impressed me as a compassionate man. On the other hand, his partner, Dr. Erhardt, whom I hadn't met, struck both Diane and Dad as harshly abrupt when they spoke to him.

Our discussion had been especially clinical, very professional. Then, Dr. Johnstone asked me how the other members of our family were holding up. I explained that it was a terrible strain, because my sister had terminal cancer, and that she had recently taken a turn for the worse, was hospitalized, and could not get down to Florida. I went on to say that this was just horrible because Nancy and Mom had such a special relationship. The next thing I knew, I was sobbing loudly and uncontrollably. Dr. Johnstone sat startled in his chair; while Dr. Patel quickly jumped from behind his desk, put his arm around me, and spoke words of assurance. While I felt terribly embarrassed at suddenly, completely losing my grip, it was a relief to expend all the pent-up emotion. I had been struggling with my sadness ever since Nancy first came down with cancer, three years earlier; and I had been feeling awful over the previous few weeks; but over the entire three years, I had never shed any more than a few tears. Now, the dam had finally broken.

Mom was awake when we arrived at the hospital. Dad and I were with her and she wasted no time in letting us know her decision.

"Bill, I've decided to give the dialysis a try. After all, the doctors think that I might still have a chance; and if it doesn't work, we'll just pull the plug."

I swallowed hard as I listened, because I had no clue as to how successful we might be in trying to remove Mom from dialysis. But, it wasn't the time to raise the issue.

Fortunately, Dr. Rodriguez stopped by Mom's room soon afterwards. When speaking alone with him, he expressed views very similar to those previously shared by Dr. Patel when Mom went on the respirator. He acknowledged that Mom was very sick; but he pointed out that he had seen a few patients recuperate from conditions as severe as her. Given Mom's will to live and demonstrated ability to bounce back on the respirator, acute dialysis seemed to him like a wise choice. When I pressed him on being able to remove Mom from dialysis should her condition continue to deteriorate, he assured me that he would make no attempts to sustain Mom if she could not live productively, even though "productively" might involve chronic dialysis, perhaps involving trips to a clinic twice a week. Given Mom's frail condition, I was skeptical about the chronic dialysis. However, I liked Dr. Rodriguez very much: and found myself agreeing with him when he said, "Let's try this for three or four days, and see the effects."

Unfortunately, time was pressing in on Diane and me. It was approaching the end of the week, and we had to leave on Sunday in order for us both to get to work and for the kids to return to school. I had been away for nearly two weeks, and I couldn't justify any further absence, especially given the fact that it wasn't at all clear how Mom's condition was going to resolve itself. Recovery would take time. Death from uremic poisoning would be agonizingly slow.

Soon after coming off of the respirator, Mom had been moved to a single room out of the Cardiac Intensive Care Unit. In the new room, she was allowed fairly constant visitation, except for when she was receiving her dialysis treatments. Her first treatment was on Friday, and the results were not encouraging. The process was far more draining than we had realized it would be. Mom, the ultimate stoic, acknowledged how tough it was lying still through the several-hour procedure. Going into dialysis, Mom was terribly lethargic. Coming out, she seemed much worse. She was totally exhausted. But when I questioned him about Mom's condition, Dr. Rodriguez assured me that such a response was typical and that it would take multiple treatments over several days to see real improvement, if there would be any improvement. He also acknowledged that the strain could throw Mom back into heart failure. Immediately after completing that first treatment, Mom checked in with her own opinion. While drifting off to sleep, she cracked, "This is a hell of a price to pay, but if I have to do it to get better, I will."

When she awoke, Mom suddenly began projectile vomiting dark brown stomach fluids. Sitting by her bedside, Dad and I were caught totally by surprise. I was in a chair next to Mom, and Dad was at the foot of the bed, when she spontaneously erupted. Poor Dad nearly went into shock, later confessing to me that, "I was sure your mother was dying right on the spot." Caught completely off guard, I rang for the nurse; then began cleaning up Mom, all the while asking her if she felt alright and if there was anything else I could do. We later learned that the vomiting was another symptom of advancing uremic poisoning, and that we could expect additional occurrences.

Saturday was a critical day. Diane, the kids and I were going to have to leave early the next morning, and we desperately hoped for some improvement before taking off. However, there was no sign of kidney function throughout the day. Following her afternoon dialysis, Mom, who threw up twice more, just wanted to sleep. Yet somehow, that evening, she was a bit more alert, and we had the opportunity to say our good-byes. All of the kids trooped in, and Mom put on her best face for them. Then I took them off for a while, so Diane and Mom could have some time alone. After which, Diane did the same for me, taking Dad and the kids back to Vista del Lago and allowing me to linger.

I was certain that this would be the last time that I would ever see Mom alive. Although her voice was halting, she marshaled enough energy for us to have a lengthy conversation, roaming over a wide range of topics. Mostly, I listened. Occasionally, I asked a question regarding something about which I was particularly curious.

"I am so glad that I lived to see you turn forty, be married and have children. Diane is such a sweet person, and you have a wonderful family. All that money that we spent sending you to Dickinson was the best investment that we ever made. Even if you hadn't finished, it would have been worth it just to meet Diane!

"You bet! Mom, it's good to see you so up, even though you're this sick. Have you ever in your life gotten really depressed?"

"Maybe once. It was after Bill Smith died, and before I married your father. Nancy was still ill from the polio, and I started to feel real sorry for myself. Then I woke up one morning and decided that I didn't like feeling that way, and I was never going to again."

"Got any tips for me?"

"Relax! Don't let yourself get all stressed out. And about your work, don't worry about those old farts who don't pay enough attention to what you know about teaching medical students. You're right. They can't learn by being lectured to all the time. It's too much stuff to cram into their heads. Things will change…"

"What do you think about heaven?"

"I think that heaven is right here on earth. I think that you make your own heaven. It's what you do here that counts. But if I do go somewhere afterwards, I hope that I don't run into Bill Smith. He'll give me a hard time..."

"Do you know that when they brought you to the hospital, you claimed that you were seeing elephants?"

"I really did see an elephant. It was right as I was coming in. I looked up, saw it, and asked what it was; and they said, 'A sick elephant!' But there wasn't actually an elephant, was there?"

"I don't know. I wasn't there. You know, Mom, I've got to go, but I'm having a terribly hard time leaving. I don't want to go back to Tennessee, but I've got to get back and do some work, if I still want to have a job."

"I know, Donn. Don't feel bad. I really appreciate all that you have done to help out, and your father will be OK. Aunt Ruth will keep an eye on him. You know, I've had seventy-five good years, and you can't ask for any more than that. Of course seventy-five isn't all that old, but I've had a wonderful life. I have nothing but good memories. If I had any bad ones, I've washed them all away. There are a lot of things worse in life than death."

"Thanks for everything, Mom. You've been the greatest."

"Thank you too, Donn. I'm really glad that you're my son."

I leaned over the bed rail, kissed Mom on the forehead, told her I loved her, and, eyes misting, headed toward the doorway. As I turned to say good-bye one more time, Mom called out.

"Good luck with you career. I'll be so proud of you. I just won't be here to know it!"

I laughed out loud. As she had so often over the years, Mom had managed to cheer me up by getting in just the right quip. I told her one more time that I loved her, walked out the door and down the hallway. I entered an exterior stairwell, descended one flight of steps, and burst into tears.

As we drove north on Rt. 95, I was surreally detached. The boys bantered about everything imaginable, from the probabilities of countless different baseball players eventually making it into the Hall of Fame, to whether or not David and Philip had played with Pretty Ponies and Barbie Dolls when they were Jenny's age. Meanwhile, Diane and I tried to have our own conversation about how things had gone in Florida and what we would be confronting over the next few weeks. But, while participating in all the talk, I remained deeply preoccupied with the thought of never seeing Mom again.

Although I knew there was still a slim chance that she might pull through this episode, the probability seemed so small, and the sense of loss saddened me immensely. Still, somehow I also felt blessedly privileged because Mom and I had shared such frank and loving talks over the last few weeks. There was great comfort in the fact that nothing had been left unsaid. Simultaneously, I felt horribly sad for all who never had the opportunity to experience closure with those they love; and I felt especially tormented about Nancy's inability to travel to Florida. After Mom had gotten out of the ICU, they could talk on the telephone, but the physical separation had to be horrendously difficult for both of them. I prayed repeatedly that Mom could hang on long enough for Nancy to recover sufficiently to make the trip.

Then, over the next several days, the miraculous happened. First, Mom began responding to the acute dialysis, and soon the nephrologists felt certain that she could be discharged from the hospital and function reasonably well supported by chronic dialysis, perhaps twice a week. Given the option, Mom chose to accept the surgical insertion of a shunt necessary for her to receive the ongoing dialysis treatments. But the morning they came to insert the shunt into her arm, her lab tests revealed that, while one kidney remained useless, her other had begun functioning sufficiently well on its own. She would not need dialysis at all! Within a week Mom was home, walking around, and talking cheerfully to me on the telephone. Furthermore, Nancy flew down to Florida to spend a week. When she got there, they had an incredibly good time. Mom wasn't up to prolonged shopping, but they drove all over the area and went out to dinner several times with Dad and Aunt Ruth. Later recounting their exploits, Mom gleefully chided me.

"I told Nancy, ' Won't Donn be surprised. He's already said all his goodbyes!'"

Mom & Dad

7

"THE GREAT STORM IS OVER"

Our respite was short-lived. Within a few weeks of Nancy's visit, Dr. Johnstone recommended that Mom undergo cardiac catherization to determine the full extent of her artery blockages. Also, her nephrologists wanted to "balloon" the artery to her one functioning kidney to improve its blood flow. Mom underwent the catherization, got the kidney work done, and then had triple by-pass heart surgery, which nearly killed her. Within twenty-four hours of the coronary operation, Mom was not responding well at all. Her physicians determined that there was a blood clot close to her heart. They immediately re-opened her chest and removed the clot.

The surgery was performed at a Seventh Day Adventist hospital in Orlando; about a three hour drive from Mom and Dad's place in Stuart. Through it all, Dad stayed in a nearby motel room. Neither Bill nor I went down to Florida. Instead, we closely monitored the situation by telephone, each calling several times a day. When I finally got a chance to talk to Mom after her second heart operation, she sounded as weak as she had at the lowest point of her earlier kidney failure. I thought, "Damn it! How much of this can she take?" But slowly and surely, throughout

July, she began gaining ground. Her weight, which dropped to about ninety-five pounds on a five foot five frame designed for about 120, crept upward as she repeatedly drank enriched milkshakes. Her exercise, initially extraordinarily limited, steadily increased as she squeezed sponge rubber balls and pumped away on a tiny peddling machine. By mid-summer, though by her own account "still skinny as a rail," she sounded chipper again.

"More lives than a cat," I told her in a phone conversation.

"Sometimes it seems that way," she laughed back.

I called Mom and Dad every day, until mid-July when I felt comfortable cutting back to about twice a week. On the other hand, I continued talking to Nancy virtually every day from the time of Mom's first hospitalization until Diane, the kids and I went on vacation in mid–August. For one reason or another Nancy's surgery kept getting put off, and she began hinting that she might not need it at all. Clearly, she wasn't sharing the full story, but it seemed best not to pressure her for details about her condition. Nancy obviously wanted to control the flow of information about her disease. Our conversations were enjoyable, but there were occasional awkward, silent moments. It sometimes seemed like we were both thinking, "Well, what should we be talking about today?"

I was pleased when, late in the spring, Lynn moved home from her apartment in Philadelphia in order to help Nancy and Bub. Lynn had planned to be married in June, but when she had serious doubts about the relationship, she canceled the wedding plans, then broke off her engagement completely. Although there was a good chance that Nancy would never get to see Lynn be married, she confessed that she was pleased that Lynn wasn't rushing into an unstable relationship; and also, given her illness, greatly relieved not to be planning a wedding.

In late June, Diane and I made a trip to New Jersey to drop David and Philip off at Diane's folks for a week. After getting them secure, we took the opportunity to stop and see Nancy, Bub and Lynn in Ocean City for a brief weekend visit. We arrived on a Friday evening about 8:00 PM and left early Sunday morning to return to Tennessee.

Although Nancy didn't stray beyond the front porch and back deck of their house, she was in good spirits; and wearing a well-coifed wig, looked great. While there, Diane and I ran in the mornings, went to the beach with Lynn, Jenny and Bub Saturday afternoon and took Jenny in her stroller on the boardwalk on Saturday night. All of this activity was distributed around pleasant meals and chats with Nancy whenever we were at the house. Fortunately, we packed as much into that short visit as we possibly could. It was the last time that we would ever visit Nancy and Bub in Ocean City.

In August, Diane, the kids and I headed off on a two and one-half week, westward trip, tacking some business for me on the end of a couple of weeks of vacation. We drove across country to the Grand Canyon, then on to Fresno, California to visit Diane's brother, Dick, his pregnant wife, Nancy, and their son, Richard. Next, we visited Diane's sister Susan, her husband, Frank, and son, Andrew, at their summer cabin in the Sawtooth Mountains of Idaho.

Then we passed through Yellowstone National Park, while heading to Minneapolis, where I interviewed several individuals at the University of Minnesota College of Medicine involved in an innovative family practice, rural internship program.

Immediately before departing, I phoned Nancy and told her that I would call her a few times along the way. We were in Fresno when I first tried reaching her in Philadelphia, only to get an answering machine. She might have been anywhere, but I tried Ocean City and got another machine. I repeated calls to both homes throughout the day, always with the same result. Eventually, the pattern struck me as strange, so I placed a call to Aunt Mary to see if she knew Nancy's whereabouts.

"She's in the hospital, Donn. She was admitted yesterday, and she's having surgery tomorrow. This is going to be so upsetting for her." "What do you mean?"

"Well, she knows how you worry about her, and she didn't want this to spoil your vacation."

It was the same old Nancy! I placed a call to her hospital room. "Well, I finally tracked you down."

"How did you know I was here?"

"After trying both houses about five times, I took the hint that things weren't quite normal. So, I called Aunt Mary. Hey, how you doing?"

"Oh," (beginning to cry) "I didn't want this to happen while you were on your trip, but my oncologist felt that it was time."

"Ah, Nancy. You don't have to worry about me. I can take it. You just take good care of yourself. Do everything you can to get through this okay."

"I will."

"Does Mom know that you're having the surgery?"

"Yeah, she does. She called me earlier in the day, and she sounds alright."

"Of course! I'm amazed at the way she's bouncing back."

"She's making noises about wanting to come up here, but she's still too weak."

"Maybe once you're home, and settled down again. You don't need guests right now."

"You can say that again."

"Listen, when is the surgery?"

"Tomorrow morning."

Well, good luck. I'll be praying for you, and I'll touch base with Lynn to see how things went. I'll call you in a few days after you've got your strength back. Okay?

"Okay, Donn."

"I love you, Nancy."

"I love you too."

I quickly called Mom to talk over the whole situation. Having already "said our good-byes," our relationship was at a whole new level of comfort and honesty. We both knew that we were talking about the doctors just trying to buy Nancy additional time, but we didn't dwell on it. Mom talked about her own recovery; how bypass surgery was like "getting hit by a truck," but how once you started to come around, it made you feel so much better. She was focused on regaining her strength and getting up to Philadelphia as soon as possible, and she told me how she and Dad would stay with Aunt Mary, so they wouldn't be a burden on Nancy and Bub. "Besides," she pointed out, "Aunt Mary and Dad seem to be getting along better in their old age, and she'll enjoy having the company."

Nancy's surgery went reasonably well; and, characteristically, she chose to act as though she would make a full recovery. Like Frazier fighting Ali, no matter how much punishment she was handed, she kept moving forward.

When we returned from our trip, I talked myself out of immediately going up to Philadelphia. Having just driven cross country and back in under three weeks, we were all exhausted. I had no vacation left, and figured that Nancy wouldn't want me hovering around appearing to be expecting the worst. So, I called every few days; and relied on Lynn, Scott and Bub to keep me posted as to how Nancy was doing.

Soon it was October, and Mom and Dad traveled north. Staying with Aunt Mary in the evenings, they spent much of each day at Nancy and Bub's; where Mom helped Lynn clean, prepare meals and greet Nancy's parade of visiting friends. Most of the time, Nancy received her visitors in her bedroom, where she was increasingly confined. Dad, practicing his own form of self-imposed confinement, watched lots of TV in the den. Two weeks before Thanksgiving, Diane the kids and I made a trip up north. We went to New Jersey to visit with Dick, Nancy and their kids, Richard and newborn Bobby, who were east from California staying with Diane's parents. Along the way, we stopped in to see Nancy. We kept the visit brief, because the following week the boys and I were returning for Edie and Bill's son, Ray's, wedding to his fiancée, Kathy. Diane and Jenny would be forgoing the second trip, because Diane was locked into giving a workshop for teachers in Tennessee.

Nancy and Her Grandson, Scottie, November, 1990

The great moment of the first visit was seeing Nancy holding her first grandchild, Scottie, Scott's and his wife, Karen's, newborn son. She beamed as she cradled him in her arms; causing me to think, "Thank God. The chemotherapy and the surgery have all been worth it, no matter what the cost!" I was equally grateful for the fact that Mom was still alive and there with Nancy. It was so fitting, since they had been through so much together. Finally, it was deeply comforting that Lynn had returned home to nurse her mother at the end. The rough times they had experienced when Lynn was a teenager were ancient history.

The toughest part of the visit was dealing with Nancy's physical deterioration. Her life-long act of masking her disabilities had now become a telephone trick. On the phone, she made herself sound great, but since our visit in June she had declined dramatically. Her cancer had spread to her liver, and her complexion was grayish. She was gaunt, the signs of resilience gone from her body. We talked as she sat in bed, her thinning hair wrapped in a white, terry cloth turban matching her oversized robe. I was shaken by her obvious weakness; but we had no time alone with each other, so I didn't broach the topic of how she felt about her condition. There was no opportunity for serious discussion.

As we pulled away from Nancy and Bub's, I looked forward to return-ing the following week and spending more time with Nancy. Although the twenty-four hours of round-trip driving to Tennessee was tiring, time was running out. Each opportunity to visit had to be seized and savored. All the way up the Jersey Turnpike to Diane's parents' house, I was haunted by Nancy's sickly image, and the thought that there could be no miraculous comeback this time. On the outside, I appeared okay, but within I was shattered. When we got to Diane's parents, the joyous greetings of a different family gathering were totally out of synch with my emotional state. I pressed on, laughing through the hustle and bustle of Diane's family setting the table and then eating supper. But throughout the meal, I sat, self-absorbed, thinking, "Don't you all realize she is dying! She is dying! My sister is dying!"

Somewhere along the line, I got up from the table, walked towards the downstairs den and completely lost it, crying uncontrollably. Diane and our sister-in-law, Nancy, a nurse, came running and began comforting me. Then came Diane's brother, Dick, a physician. As I sobbed, I was suddenly struck by the strange irony of being attended to by my two in-laws, Nancy and Dick, who had the same first names as my own Nancy and her first husband. But the coincidence didn't stop there. Nancy Thistle's maiden name was Smith, the same as Nancy's before she was adopted by my father; and Nancy Thistle's father's name was Bill Smith, the same as my sister's biological father. As much as the caring support that I was receiving, recognizing this strange twist helped me pull myself back together. I laughed at the cosmic joke that God seemed to be playing on me.

In one week, I was again back at Nancy's bedside. After the boys had a little time to visit, we had an opportunity to talk alone. "So, how you feeling, Nancy?"

"Really, not too bad. I get tired; but otherwise I do pretty well, once I'm a few days past the chemotherapy."

"But you're not getting around too much anymore."

No. This is pretty much it for now. Every once in a while I go down to the den, but it tires me out. Once I start getting my strength back, I'll go downstairs more."

I swallowed hard and plunged into where I felt I had to go. "Nancy, have you given any thoughts to arranging for hospice care? One of my friends, you remember Rick Loerch's wife, Trish, found her local hospice to be wonderful for her and for her family."

"Hospice! Oh, no." She said laughing. "Hospices are for people who are dying!"

And there it was. Nancy was not going to go there. She

stopped me short in my tracks. My friend Trish, who died of liver cancer, and I had shared a lengthy conversation about her impending death. She had achieved a level of acceptance that was comforting to her and to others. Nancy, on the other hand, was determined that she was going to battle death right down to the end. I sat next to her, holding her hand, speechless, not having a clue what to say next. Then Nancy spoke. "I want to show you something. It's a fax that someone sent to me. There's a copy of it over on my desk. Go get it, would ya."

I fetched the fax, returned to the chair next to Nancy's bed, and read the contents.

IF YOU ARE UNHAPPY

Once upon a time, there was a nonconforming
   sparrow who decided not to fly south for the winter.
   However, soon the weather turned so cold that he reluctantly started to fly south.
   In a short time ice began to form on his wings and he fell to earth in a barnyard, almost frozen.
   A cow passed by and crapped on the little sparrow, the sparrow thought it was the end. But the manure warmed him and defrosted his wings.
   Warm and happy, able to breathe, he started to sing.
   Just then a large cat came by and hearing the chirping, investigated the sounds.
   The cat cleared away the manure, found the chirping bird and promptly ate him.

THE MORAL OF THE STORY:

   1. *Everyone who craps on you is not necessarily your enemy.*

2. *Everyone who gets you out of crap is not necessarily your friend.*
3. *And, if you're warm and happy in a pile of crap, keep your mouth shut.*

"Isn't that hilarious?" Nancy asked with a wry, but pained, smile on her face.

I was amused, but taken aback, my mind racing as I considered my answer. Nothing could have caught me more off guard than the dung-laced parable underscoring Nancy's desire not to talk about her plight. Even though I had often reflected on how Nancy's extended childhood bout with polio taught her to relentlessly push forward without self-pity, I remained baffled by her refusal to let go so near the end. Ever-so-briefly, the thought crossed my mind that perhaps Nancy didn't know how close she was to death; but I couldn't believe that. She was too smart. I guessed that something else was going on; that Nancy, always better at giving than receiving, had decided that keeping up the brave front was how she would continue helping others. This struck me as misguided, but Nancy had chosen her course, and I was going to have to accept it. It would be cruelly selfish of me to insist on anything different. This was her death not mine.

"Yeah, Nancy." I laughed, "I guess that just about says it all."

She looked satisfied. On the other hand, I felt that we had come up short, even though I had been taught a valuable lesson about how different we all are. We chatted a while longer, and I explained that we would be staying in Tennessee for Thanksgiving. Two weeks of travel in a row had taken their toll on me and on the boys, and we needed to stay put for a bit rather than to return to Philadelphia the upcoming Thursday to celebrate with family.

"I'll see you at Christmas," I said, just before leaning over and kissing her good-bye. I love you, Nancy."

"I love you too. You drive carefully, and give Diane and Jenny both big hugs from me."
"Will do."
"Remember, drive carefully."
"Okay. I will. Bye!"
"Bye!"

Over the next few weeks, I talked to Nancy and Mom on the phone several times. They both told me that Thanksgiving had been a special occasion, with everyone taking their dinner up to Nancy's room to eat with her. Meanwhile, I filled them in on my latest professional distraction. I was a finalist for an assistant dean's position at Ohio University's College of Medicine in Athens, Ohio. I loved the town. The work seemed good, the people were great; and if the offer was made before a state-mandated hiring freeze, I was pretty sure the job was mine. So, I was excited about the possibilities, and was sitting at the kitchen table one night staring intently at an Ohio University campus map, when the phone rang. Diane picked it up.

"Donn, it's Scott. He wants to talk to you."

"Thanks, Honey."

Reaching for the phone, I guessed that Nancy was very close to death, and this was a call to return home. I braced myself, and began calculating how to get us all up to Philadelphia as soon as possible.

"Donn!"

"Hey, Scott. How's Nancy doing?"

"This is Scott."

"Yeah, Scott I know."

"Donn."

"Yeah, Scott."

"Mom died around 11:00 this morning."

"Oh, God!...No!...Oh, No! No!...God, No!" I cried. "I was so sure...sure that she would live through Christmas. I just wanted to see her one more time. We'd have come up for Thanksgiving, but....but I had no idea."

"None of us did. She seemed okay yesterday, but this morning she complained about not feeling well. Then she just sat up in bed and said she had to get to the hospital quickly. Lynn and Bub called an ambulance and got her to Chestnut Hill Hospital, but she wasn't there all that long before she died. Not even the doctors figured it was coming."

"How are you all doing?"

"It's been pretty rough."

"How's Bub?"

"He took it really hard. He wasn't with Mom when she died. She seemed comfortable; so he and Lynn ran home to take showers and get dressed, cause they were still in their pajamas. When they came back, Mom was already dead."

"Was anyone with her?"

"Yeah, me...MomMom and PopPop were at the hospital, but they were off getting something to eat."

"I'm sure it was tough, Scott; but I'm so glad that you were able to be with her. Did she say anything at the end?"

"Not really. She was pretty uncomfortable. I could tell that she was in trouble, and I called for a nurse. I held her hand, and told her that I loved her. She said she loved me too. That was pretty much it. She started breathing real heavy, and then stopped breathing completely."

"My, God! How are MomMom and PopPop?"

"They're holding together. They're upset, but they seem okay. I guess they knew it was coming sooner or later."

"Yeah, but you still think that there's going to be more time." Scott was calling from Nancy and Bub's house. He put Bub on the phone, and we talked for a little while. Bub had regained his composure since the morning and was very attentive to my feelings, aware that I was the one who was getting the shocking news. Meanwhile, I struggled to find comforting words to say to him, but found myself fumbling around. Amidst my sobs, I told him how sad I was for him, and how much I appreciated the fact that he had stood by and cared for Nancy, throughout her illness. Pulling myself together, we discussed the funeral plans. Diane and I would have three days to get things straightened out in Tennessee to get up to Philadelphia for an evening viewing.

> Cem., Camden. No eve. viewing. Visitation will begin 11:30 A.M., Thurs. at the Funeral Home. If desired memorial contributions may be made to American Heart Assn., 600 White Horse Pike, Audubon, N.J. 08106 or Marine Mammal Stranding Center, P.O. Box 773, Brigantine, N.J. 08203 in memory of Mr. DuBell.
>
> **FLANAGAN**
> Dec. 3, 1990, of Wyndmoor, Pa., NANCY W. (nee Weinholtz), beloved wife of Albert P. (Bub), loving mother of Lynn A. Hornbaker and Scott P. Hornbaker; also survived by one grandson, Scott P. Hornbaker, Jr. and daughter of William and Agatha Weinholtz, stepmother of Albert P. Jr., Jacqueline C. and Brian M. Flanagan and sister of Donn and William Weinholtz, Jr. Relatives and friends are invited to the funeral Fri., 9 A.M., at THE McILVAINE FUNERAL HOME, 3711 Midvale Ave. Funeral service 11 A.M., at the Presbyterian Church of Chestnut Hill, 8855 Germantown Ave. Int. Westminster Cem. Friends may call Thurs. eve. at the Funeral Home, 7 to 9. In lieu of flowers donations in Nancy's name to The American Cancer Society or The March of Dimes appreciated.
>
> **GALLOP**
> PATRICK J. SR., on Dec. 3, 1990, of Glenolden, Pa., husband of Marie (nee Bibb), father of Capt. David L., Lt. Patrick J. Jr., and Ens. Robert J. Gallop, brother

Nancy's Obituary, 1990

Rather than making a single twelve-hour trip, we broke it up into two half-days; arriving at Aunt Mary's, where we stayed along with Mom andDad, about 4:00 PM on the day of the viewing. We hustled in, grabbed some dinner, changed our clothes, and headed into Philadelphia to the funeral parlor. We had no reservations about taking the boys to the viewing, but Jenny was so young, three, that Aunt Mary arranged for a babysitter to take care of her.

Seeing Nancy lying in her casket painfully dramatized death's finality, and I dwelled on how terribly much I was going to miss her. Then, desperately groping for a lighter side, smiled at the thought that, by outliving her, Bill and I might someday both be older than Nancy was when she died, thereby making us her "older" brothers. Nancy might get a kick out of this because she had always kidded Bill about looking older than her. I found some small refuge in the fact that Nancy was being spared aging's relentless physical decline, and that she would always be remembered for her energy and playfulness, the final few months of her life being only a brief anomaly.

Bub, Lynn and Scott received visitors at home following the viewing. Mom and Dad went, but Diane and I, exhausted from the trip north, returned with Aunt Mary to her house to put our kids, and ourselves, to bed. The next morning, I got up to take an early morning run before eating breakfast and getting dressed for the funeral. The December air was crisp and cold. It calmed me; satisfying my endorphin addiction and causing me to reflect on miles and miles of running, going all the way back to when I started at age fifteen, the year Nancy, Lynn and Scott first moved in with us.

Later that morning, we packed ourselves into our Plymouth Voyager minivan, Diane giving up her front seat, so Mom, still painfully thin following her summer coronary bypass, would be more comfortable on the way to the funeral. Dad and Aunt Mary sat in the middle seat, and Diane moved to the back with the boys. Jenny again stayed home with a sitter. After we were all in the car, I told Mom that there was something that I wanted everyone to listen to. It was a cut of Bob Franke's *The Great Storm Is Over* from folk singer John McCuthcheon's album, *Water From Another Time*. McCutcheon had sung the song at his own mother's funeral. As we drove along, his voice rang out, first softly, then powerfully.

The thunder and lightning gave voice to the night. The little lost child
cried aloud in her fright. Hush, little baby, a story I will tell
Of a love that has vanquished the powers of hell.
Al—le—lu—ia, the great storm is over,
Lift up your wings and fly.
Al—le—lu—ia, the great storm is over,
Lift up your wings and fly.
Sweetness in the air and justice on the wind. Laughter in the house
where the mourners had been. The deaf shall have music, the blind have
new eyes. The standards of death taken down by surprise.
Al—le—lu—ia, the great storm is over,
Lift up your wings and fly.
Al—le—lu—ia, the great storm is over,
Lift up your wings and fly.
Release for the captives, an end to the wars. Streams in the desert, new
hope for the poor. The little lost children shall dance as they sing. And
play with the bears and the lions in spring.
Al—le—lu—ia, the great storm is over,
Lift up your wings and fly.
Al—le—lu—ia, the great storm is over,
Lift up your wings and fly.
Hush, little baby, let go of your fears.
The Lord loves his own and your mother is here. The babe fell asleep as
the lantern did burn.
The mother kept singing till her bridegroom's return.
Al—le—lu—ia, the great storm is over, Lift up your wings and fly.
Al—le—lu—ia, the great storm is over, Lift up your wings and fly.

While the song played, I glanced at Mom, who virtually never cried. Tears were in her eyes. She gave an approving nod, paused, then spoke. "I never thought that Nancy would even live to be a teenager. I feel so fortunate that we had her for fifty-three years."

Although Nancy had been attending Catholic Mass since marrying Bub, as a divorcee, she was unable to convert to Catholicism. So, her funeral was held just outside of Philadelphia at the Chestnut Hill Presbyterian Church; our family's church when I was a very young child. Though located in a mid-Atlantic state, it's the kind of church you would expect to find in the middle of a New England town; large with an elegant steeple and clean white paint. I hadn't set foot in the sanctuary for over thirty years, but it immediately felt like home.

The place was packed. Looking around, I wondered, "What did Nancy ever do to attract so many people?"

Then, I began longing for a Quaker memorial service, where all who have been touched by the deceased are invited to speak as they feel deeply moved. I wanted so much to hear what those present might say about Nancy, and I yearned for my own opportunity to speak. Knowing that we were in for a more traditional, scripted Protestant ceremony, I resigned myself to accepting a poor substitute. After all, the minister didn't even know Nancy. What kind of eulogy could he offer?

Then, following the hymns and prayers, Associate Pastor David Poland showed me just how wrong I could be.

"I would like to begin by thanking you, the family and friends of Nancy Flanagan, for allowing me the privilege of conducting her funeral service. If that sounds a bit odd coming from the officiating pastor, then please let me explain.

Nancy

"I never got to know Nancy personally, but in the past few days have become acquainted with her through you. You had the benefit of sharing in her life, in her joys and trials, in her tears and laughter. And, from the things you have told me about Nancy, I have come to envy you for that, for I have heard that Nancy Flanagan was a wonderful companion. She felt things very deeply, and she gave herself unselfishly to many people. She was truly a caring person, whose influence and memory will live at least as long as you do."

"Death was a word that did not seem to be in Nancy's vocabulary. Call it denial, call it courage, call it what you will…Nancy didn't want to talk about it, as though death was simply not an option for her. And maybe that's not all bad; perhaps that attitude or outlook was a major factor in what kept her going, even against the odds, these past three or four years. Nancy Flanagan lived a victorious life. Although she became afflicted with polio a year before the vaccine for that malady was developed, she was a determined, positive-thinking person. Other people in her condition might consider themselves handicapped, but this was just another word that wasn't in Nancy's vocabulary. She wasn't a complainer, but rather was always interested in other people. She was a Welcome Wagon hostess for several years, recently organized her high school class's 35th year reunion, and actively worked for the Cancer Society and March of Dimes as a volunteer. It seems to me that she set some good examples that we might do well to follow. Her good sense of humor and positive attitude no doubt shielded many people from knowing the full extent of her illness. In short, Nancy's example gives new meaning, as her family points out, to the word "courage," no doubt the single most outstanding word that was in her vocabulary."

"For my part, I shall look forward to meeting you one day, Nancy, in God's house of many mansions, where the roads of all faith meet. Until then, my friend,

May the road rise to meet you;

may the wind be always at your back; may the sun shine warm upon your face, the rain fall softly on your fields.

And until we meet again,

may God hold you in the palm of his hand."

8

I'D RATHER GO OUT SMILING

Mom did amazingly well over the next three years. She had to so she could take care of Dad, who suffered his stroke in March of 1991, just four months after Nancy died. Fittingly, it came after a day on the golf course. Dad always said that he wanted to die immediately after finishing a round of golf. Nearly getting his wish, he finished his game, came home, made himself a sandwich, sat down on the screened-in back porch of their 2nd floor condominium, began the New York Times Cross Word Puzzle, and experienced a partially paralyzing stroke.

While Dad was making his sandwich in the kitchen, Mom settled down to read on a small, back porch, loveseat. She dozed off to sleep soon after Dad sat down in his chair on the porch, later awakening and realizing something was terribly wrong when Dad didn't respond to her questions. Instead, he sat still in his chair, staring blankly out the back window at the lake behind their apartment building. Mom got up and stood directly in front of him. Dad tried to speak to her, but he couldn't. She called an ambulance, which took him to a hospital.

True to form, Mom had everything pretty much under control by the time she contacted Bill and me.

"Donn, Dad had a small stroke yesterday. The doctors say that it was 'serious,' but that it could have been much worse. It's going to slow him down for a while, but he should make a pretty good recovery."

"Oh my God, Mom. How's he doing? How bad is it?"

"Well, he can't talk much at all right now, and he has trouble walking, but the doctors say that he'll begin to be able to do both pretty soon. They're going to release him from the hospital in a few days, and we'll have visiting nurses and occupational therapists come to work with him and get him functioning again."

"How are you?"

"Oh, you know me. I'm okay. I'm a lot stronger than I was at Christmas. All of that pedaling and squeezing those rubber balls is paying off. And we have so much support down here. The health care system is really set up to take care of old folks who are starting to fall apart, and Aunt Ruth is a big help."

We further discussed Dad's condition for a while. Then I announced my plans.

"Listen, when is Dad supposed to get out of the hospital?"

"Probably Thursday."

"I'll be down on Friday night. I'll probably bring one of the kids with me, so Diane doesn't have to deal with all three of them. We'll leave early in the morning, and maybe be there by 9:00."

"Donn, you don't have to do that."

"Yeah, I know I don't, but that's what I want to do. I'll feel a lot better. I want to see Dad, and let him see me. Okay?"

"Okay. It'll be good for everyone. You're right. It will make Dad happy. But don't be too upset when you see him. He'll be much better in a few months. That's the way these strokes are."

Diane and I decided that Phil would go with me. He was approaching seven at the time, about the age that David was when he and I traveled to Ocean City to visit Nancy. We knew Phil would be good company for me, and we didn't want Dave to think he would always be tapped to visit folks when they were seriously ill.

Our trip got off to an unsettling start. About forty miles from Johnson City, Phil developed a bad stomach ache and diarrhea, requiring several bathroom stops and about a ninety minute delay. But otherwise things went pretty smoothly, and we pulled into Vista Del Lago around 10:30 PM. Mom was dressed and waiting for us. Dad had been sleeping, but Mom awakened him when we arrived. We were in their apartment living room for about five minutes before Dad came out to greet us. Decked out in his normal sleeping regalia, boxer shorts and a sleeveless T-shirt, Dad looked at first glance like his old normal self; trim for a seventy-six year old with surprisingly good muscle tone. But upon closer inspection, reality quickly set in. One side of Dad's face was noticeably drooped; his gait was unsteady; and his speech was slurred. Although he looked happy to see us, he also looked deeply embarrassed at his condition. As Phil and I hugged him, I wondered if there would be any more strokes and just how full his recovery could be.

He surprised me. Within six months, Dad looked fine; and when talking to him, the only lingering effects appeared to be occasional inability to recall a name or a particular word. If he hadn't become so visibly frustrated at these lapses, they might have passed as typical "senior moments." Less apparent, though, was a permanent loss of initiative that caused him to give up his beloved golf, and to no longer offer Mom any help around the house. Since Dad had been remarkably attentive to all of the household chores following her hospitalizations, for Mom this was a dramatic shift, which became a nagging irritation. She would have liked Dad to at least put his dishes in the sink following a meal, or to pack his suitcase for a trip. Still, with the help of a local cleaning service and by eating out a few nights a week, they got by reasonably well; and we continued to visit them each spring and summer even after we moved to Connecticut in 1991.

On Christmas Eve of 1993, sitting across the dinner table from Mom, I noticed how frail she looked. Though still meticulously dressed and fully in command of her thoughts and speech, her wrinkles were more pronounced and her movements more cautious. She was once again hampered by a slight, but nagging, cough.

Our entire extended family was seated in a restaurant located near Edie's and Bill's house outside of Philadelphia. For two years Mom and Dad had insisted on taking us all out to dinner prior to retreating to Edie and Bill's to open presents; wanting to keep the extended family's Christmas Eve tradition alive, while sparing Edie and Bill the expense and hassle of preparing a huge meal for everyone.

As we chatted, I warned Mom that mycoplasma, or some similar bug, might be rearing its ugly head again, and that she should see about getting another prescription of erythromycin. She assured me that she would, but that she wanted to wait until she returned to Florida to see Dr. Johnstone. If the cough worsened before she got back, she would telephone him and ask him to call in a prescription to Edie and Bill's pharmacy. Then she shifted the conversation to the fact that, for the second year in a row, she and Dad would be unable to spend a portion of Christmas vacation with us in Connecticut. I understood. They had flown up north, and even if they had opted to rent a car, I didn't want them negotiating the traffic they would encounter in route to our house. So, when the evening was over, we kissed good-bye and promised to call regularly. We would see each other early in July, when Diane, Jenny and I planned to drop Dave and Phil off at camp in Tennessee, then drive on to Florida.

It didn't work out that way. By the end of January, Mom was back in the hospital with borderline congestive heart failure; her physicians making it clear to her that, if she wanted to live, she was going to require a shunt placed in her arm and become a chronic dialysis patient. Given Dad's dependence on her, her faith in the doctors who had pulled her through her previous crises, and her incredible spunk; Mom followed the physicians' recommendations.

But this time, nothing went well. Mom's overall condition had deteriorated too greatly. In spite of multiple efforts over the next several months to insert a shunt in her arm, none would "take." Instead, Mom, the stoic, experienced weeks of round-the-clock excruciating pain each time a shunt was inserted. As usual, she minimized her complaints when talking with her physicians, conveying the impression that she was experiencing tolerable discomfort.

Bill and Edie flew down in January to help Mom make the transition from the hospital back to the apartment, and I made plans to go, alone, the weekend of Dad's birthday, February sixth. Talking to me on the phone while he and Edie were down there, Bill painted a picture of Mom's acute distress.

"You know her, Donn. She doesn't complain at all. But this morning she was sitting in her chair crying at 6:00 AM. Dad and Edie were still asleep, and I got up to go to the bathroom. I heard someone in the den, and I went back to check things out. Mom didn't know that I was up, but I stood there watching her for about a minute. She was just sitting there crying. She didn't make a sound, but the tears were pouring out. Then, as soon as she realized that I was there, she stopped and pretended like she was okay. It's not good."

By the time that I reached Florida, the first shunt had come out. Mom was greatly relieved that it was gone; but she wasn't optimistic about plans to insert another within a month. It was as though she realized that a critical threshold had been crossed, and there was no turning back. Amazingly, otherwise, her attitude was good; even though she was very weak and was restricted to shuffling back and forth between her bed and the den, immediately adjacent to the bedroom. Somehow, Mom managed to be a lot of fun to be around, even when she was suffering.

On the morning of Dad's birthday, I awoke on the sofa bed in the living room to the sound of Mom's and Dad's bedroom conversation.

"Well! good morning, Dear."

"Good morning."

"And happy birthday!"

"Thank you."

"With me lying here all the time, I wasn't able to go out and get you a present."

"That's okay. I don't need any other present. I can't think of anything that I would want more than having you lying here next to me."

"Ah, thank you. You're sweet."

I laid quietly for some time, so as not to disturb them, thankful for having two parents who cared so much for each other.

Unfortunately, Diane, who was working on her doctorate at the University of Connecticut, the kids and I all had different spring vacations that year. So, it wasn't possible for us all to visit Florida in March. Instead, I again flew down by myself. By that time, the second shunt had failed and been removed. With it gone, Mom freely acknowledged that it had been terribly painful, and that she didn't hold out much hope for ever getting one successfully inserted. She hadn't been dialyzed since her last hospitalization, and her functioning kidney was barely doing its job. I realized that it wouldn't take much of an assault to kick her back into congestive heart failure and total kidney shut-down; and flew home after the several-day visit wondering just how Mom's endgame would play itself out. The next hospitalization came in May. Using medication, Mom's physicians were able to control the congestive heart failure, keeping her off of a respirator, but the kidneys were another story. Mom repeatedly underwent dialysis, using temporary shunts which were prone to infection, while the physicians sought a more permanent port.

Edie and Bill flew to Florida immediately, but I held off for a few days to attend the University of Hartford's spring graduation, knowing that, as long as Mom was receiving dialysis, she would stay alive. From talking to her on the phone, it was clear that the issue we would be facing was going to be whether or not she wanted to persist with the attempts to shift her to chronic dialysis. Under the circumstances, it seemed best for her to have plenty of time to think things through. With our commencement ceremonies on Sunday, I purchased a ticket to fly to Florida early on Monday morning.

This particular graduation was especially important to me because the University was giving an honorary degree to the commencement speaker, Theodore Sizer. Ted, a noted school reformer from Brown University and a former Dean of Education at Harvard, had nominated me for my job at the University of Hartford; and the University tapped me to present him for his honorary doctorate. Also being honored was Mary Everett, the Director of the American Occupational Therapy Association, who would be handing degrees to the first graduating class of our college's new Occupational Therapy program. Having both Ted and Mary there at the same ceremony was a real coup for us, and my colleagues and I had been anticipating the celebration for months.

During the days leading up to and including commencement, I

avoided small talk discussions which might cause me to explain everything that was going on with Mom. I just wanted to enjoy the upcoming party as best I could, then get off to Florida as quickly as possible. Other than updating my two dear friends and office assistants, Arlene Ruddy and Bev Neddermann, I kept the seriousness of Mom's condition and my trip plans to myself. Still, I couldn't let the occasion go by without paying some tribute to Mom, who I was pretty sure wouldn't be with us much longer. Focusing my address to our college's graduates on the importance of their parents to their own development, I shared a few things about my parents.

"My father taught me to love my family, to value accomplishment and to work hard in order to achieve. My mother certainly reinforced all of these qualities; but she further taught me, more often by deed than by word, about the importance of balance and harmony. From her, I learned about being in touch with myself, so I might better mesh with those around me. This is an important lesson in life, but in the helping professions it is ever so important. As educators and health professionals, we are most effective when we establish the types of relationships described by the sociologist, philosopher and theologian Martin Buber; those which involve I and Thou. To connect with Thou, I must be whole. To stay whole over a career and lifetime, I must stay balanced, in touch with myself."

"So, in an era when burnout and over-extension are constant traps, take time to care for yourselves. Nurture yourselves without being selfish. Tend to yourselves, so you may better tend to others."

"As you leave the University of Hartford, I wish you all productive, balanced careers, and productive balanced lives."

While speaking, I envisioned Mom in her hospital bed with Dad by her side. Part of me desperately wanted to say,

"Please indulge me these few minutes because my mother, who I love dearly, is dying. And I just hope that you are fortunate enough to have parents who have been as good to you as mine have been to me."

But I held off, making no direct mention to anyone, except Arlene and Bev, about how I was feeling. It pleased me to surreptitiously embed the little tribute, and I decided to describe it to Mom before she died. It would be a final, small gift to take with me to Florida.

Bill picked me up at the airport in Ft. Lauderdale. As we drove north on Interstate 95, it became clear that, while he wasn't optimistic about Mom's chances, Bill hadn't given up hope. After all, she had pulled out of these tailspins before. It just might happen again.

I clung to the same hope, but not for long. Edie, Bill and Dad gave me an opportunity to visit with Mom alone soon after we arrived at the hospital. Without prompting, Mom opened up.

"It's a racket, Donn. I tell you, it's a racket. They fill you full of tubes, and they take your money. They keep telling me that they're going to get this shunt in soon, but it never happens; and it's not going to happen."

Taken aback by Mom's attitude, which shifted dramatically to angry and impatient as soon as we were alone, I probed to better understand where she was coming from.

"Mom, are you going to pull through this, or do you have something else in mind?"

Calming down immediately, Mom spoke to my concerns, rather than continuing to vent her frustrations with the health-care system.

"Donn, I think that I am going to die. I don't think that I am going to make it this time."

"Can you hold on for a while. Diane and the kids are planning on coming down to visit in July."

"I don't think that I'll be here in July. Here's the thing! I'm not afraid of dying. I just don't like the idea of leaving Dad and you kids."

"Do you want to keep trying to make this dialysis work, or would you rather have us try to get you into a hospice."

"A hospice would be nice. Do you think you could do that?"

"I think so. All that we have to do is get the nephrologists to agree."

"I'm not sure that they are going to want to give up, but I can handle that. Every time that they have to shift one of these temporary shunts to a new place on my body, they have me sign to give them my permission. I just won't sign. They can't make me do it, as long as I am conscious and I say, 'No.'"

"Well, listen, why don't you sleep on this, and we'll see how you feel about it tomorrow. In the meantime, I'll break the news to Dad, Edie and Bill; and we'll start checking into what hospice arrangements are available; just so we can be ready if we have to."

"That sound's good. I'll think it over carefully. After all, I don't want to make a mistake about something like this. Thank you, Donn. I'm really glad that you're here."

"Me too, Mom. We all love you. We'll do everything we can do to support you. It's your call."

"I know."

A few years earlier the same conversation would have left me terribly shaken, but we had all been through so much together that I felt relatively calm and understood my responsibilities. Dad had been incapable of having a similar conversation with Mom. But when, in the visitors waiting room, I told him, along with Edie and Bill, that Mom would prefer a hospice to dialysis and further hospitalization; he looked visibly relieved and slightly energized.

"She would! She really said that. I was afraid to ask her myself. I was afraid that she would think that I didn't want her to live.

She's suffered so much. I don't want to see her suffer any more, if she doesn't want to."

"It's OK for you to talk to her about it now, Dad. She'd like to talk about it."

Dad left us to go visit with Mom, and Edie, Bill and I discussed the options. Both of them felt that it was time for us to let go of prayers for medical miracles, and to shift gears so we might help Mom to have some peaceful final days. A hospital social worker had already mentioned to Edie that she could help with arranging for hospice care, if it should ever come to that. And Edie, who like Diane was very close to Mom, was willing to follow up and see about the necessary arrangements.

Within a few hours, we learned that there were no openings currently available at any of the local hospices, but that home hospice care could be immediately arranged as an interim step. With that knowledge in hand, Dad, Edie, Bill and I retreated to a nearby restaurant, the Captain's Table, for dinner.

Having discussed hospice care with Mom, Dad seemed a changed man. He acknowledged that we wouldn't know exactly what to do until we spoke to Mom the next day, but he said that he was certain that she was not going to change her mind. He felt that it was going to be his job to protect Mom from any further medical interventions.

It was good that he and Mom had talked, because the next day her nephrologist, Dr. Erhardt, announced that it was essential for Mom to have another temporary shunt installed, replacing one in her inner thigh with one in her neck. But Mom refused to sign the authorization; where upon Dr. Erhardt, whom Dad had never much liked, spoke alone with Dad, pleading for his support. I wasn't present for the conversation; but Dad, probably overzealously, informed Dr. Erhardt that he wasn't going to allow him to cause Mom any more unnecessary pain. According to Dad, the exchange became heated before Dr. Erhardt finally turned and walked away exclaiming, "Well, if you refuse to save her, you are sacrificing her to the morphine!"

Hearing those words, made me cringe, and I assume that it had the same effect on Edie and Bill; but we all remained resolute. Consequently, by that evening we had Mom at home, in her den, in a hospital bed, and under hospice care. We had sprung her from the hospital!

Home hospice care involves daily visits by nurses who provide nurturing support, often while administering the pain medications necessary to ease the transition towards death. Still, a great deal of responsibility falls on available family members, or friends, to provide for the ongoing needs of the dying person. We knew that Dad would not be up to these demands, and that he would also need substantial emotional support. As long as Edie, Bill or I were available, there would be no problem; but renal failure involves a slow death that can stretch over a couple of weeks, and none of us could stay away from work sufficiently long to wait out such a long period. So, much to my relief, Diane offered to fly down to Florida in order to take over. I would stay until Sunday. Edie and Bill would leave on Monday morning, and Diane would arrive early Monday afternoon. In the meantime, to reduce the stress on everyone and provide Mom with maximum peace, we hoped for an opening at the Hospice of Martin, a beautiful facility serving Mom and Dad's county.

Mom always managed to generate bright smiles, even when she was hospitalized and in substantial discomfort. But those smiles took on a new radiance once she was home from the hospital. Her worn, seventy-nine year old face metamorphosed whenever she flashed her smile. Although the gradually accumulating effects of uremic poisoning increasingly caused her to doze off to sleep, while awake, she beamed and continually expressed her appreciation to us for bringing her home. After her first night back, I spoke to her about her positive attitude. "You're looking good, Mom."

"Thanks. I keep on smiling. You know I'd rather go out smiling."

"You're really quite the pragmatist, aren't you. Always thinking about next steps and never feeling sorry for yourself."

"You can't, Donn. You'd always walk around with a sad face. I remember when Nancy was sick as a child, and again years ago when your father's lung collapsed and he might have died; each time I thought, 'What am I going to do?' But I realized that you just have to pull yourself together and move on. What else can you do?"

Throughout that day, we all took turns sitting with Mom; feeding her jello or ice cream; and quietly reading while she slept. I was especially struck by how good Edie was with her. Also possessed of a glowing smile, Edie rubbed lotion on Mom's dry skin and massaged her feet, providing whatever little comforts she could. Mom's earlier illness and Nancy's death had brought Edie, Bill, Diane and me much closer together; and I deeply appreciated Edie's presence, especially since neither Diane, Lynn nor, of course, Nancy could be there.

Miraculously, we got a call that afternoon alerting us that a room was available for Mom at Hospice of Martin, and that an ambulance could transport her the following day. Mom was especially thankful. She didn't want to overly burden anyone, and she knew that if she died in the den, Dad would be haunted by the memories. As she put it,

"How's he going to sit here and enjoy watching 'Wheel of Fortune" when he's got my dead body on his mind?"

As things turned out, Mom's last night at home was a real hoot. Around 1:15 AM, we were all awakened by her calling for help. I was the first to reach the den, followed quickly by Edie and Bill. Then came Dad, who retreated to the living room as soon as he saw that Mom was alive and that we had things under control.

Mom had soiled herself, but instead of being mortified, she was laughing about it. Mockingly lamenting that she missed her bedpan, she blurted out:

"I couldn't hit the target. Put the cork back in. I must have put it in crooked. You know, now I know where the saying comes from!"

"The saying?"

"Yeah, the saying. You know, the one on the bumper stickers."

"Saying on the bumper stickers! What are you talking about, Mom?"

"You know, the one on the bumper stickers: 'Shit Happens!'"

Suddenly, we were all in stitches; two men in their underwear and a woman in her nightgown laughing hysterically as they cleaned up the dying woman who was the life of the party. And she didn't let up.

"If we had a camera, we could send this in to "America's Funniest Home Videos….Now you've seen me from every angle. It's a good thing that we're all family."

After we finished cleaning her and had kissed her good night on her forehead, Mom adopted a more serious tone. As the three of us were headed out the den door, sincerely appreciative, she said: "Thanks so much for coming right away. A lot of people would just let you lie in it."

Mom had always been the most self sufficient person that I had ever known. It had never occurred to me that one day we would get to a point where she could still be so mentally sharp, but we would have to clean her like a baby. It was no hardship for Edie, Bill and me; but the episode was very upsetting for Dad, who didn't enter the den until after Mom was clean. Looking horribly shaken, before going to sleep, he told me, "Thanks a lot, Donn. I never could have done that."

Under my breath, I thanked God that we had found a space in the hospice.

Before the ambulance arrived at noon, Edie and Bill gave Mom a bath, combed her hair, and dressed her in a bright pink blouse. Looking in a mirror for the first time in almost two months, Mom quipped,

"Not bad. If you put some rouge on me, I'd almost look alive. Now take some pictures of me before I wilt."

And so we did, with us posing around her. Things were amazingly upbeat.

When the hospice nurse and ambulance crew arrived, we got out of their way so they could do all that they had to do. Then we followed the ambulance over to the Hospice of Martin, located about twenty minutes away from Mom and Dad's place, not far from a main thoroughfare, but tucked away in a secluded area surrounded by high marsh grass.

A spread-out, one-story building, the hospice was tastefully designed and decorated. Everything about it was aesthetically pleasing; from the clean, spacious rooms with large, screened-in porches, to the choice of the furniture and the soothing colors of the walls decorated with watercolor landscapes and seascapes. Most importantly, the staff were extraordinarily supportive. As Mom was wheeled toward her room, she commented on the decor and how pleased she was with the people and the entire environment. Immediately after she was transferred into the bed in her room, she exclaimed, "I've never felt such a sense of total peace."

My only regret was a small one. Mom had always loved Florida sunsets, and had regularly told us that if she ever had a stroke, she wanted to be parked in a chair on her back porch so she could watch every sunset. But now her bed was facing east, and the screened porch with large, sliding glass doors was to her left, facing north. There would be no final, blazing sunsets for Mom to savor.

But who could complain! The hospice was far superior to what any of us had ever hoped it would be, and I thought back appreciatively on a comment Mom made to me the day before.

"Donn, I'm so glad that you came down here, and that we had a chance to talk about the hospice."

"Yeah, me too, Mom."

"And I'm glad that we've been generous in our contributions to them. It makes me not feel so bad about taking up their space."

Mom was very tired. Uremic poisoning was slowly and irreversibly taking its toll. She wanted and needed to sleep. So, we only stayed for about an hour after she settled in; then left for some lunch. We returned late in the afternoon for a while, before going out for dinner and making one last visit in the evening. These last two visits were very important to me, as I was catching an early morning flight out of Ft. Lauderdale to return to Connecticut. With Mom's certain death nearing, it was clear that I would never get to see her again.

When we came back after lunch, about 4:15 PM, Mom told us how helpful it was to speak to the hospice nurses about dying. Then we each spent some time alone with her, making sure to give Mom and Dad some extra time together by themselves, but Mom tired quickly and drifted off to sleep while each of us was with her. At about 7:00, we went to dinner at Gentleman Jim's, one of Mom and Dad's favorite places, about ten minutes away.

Not surprisingly, Dad wanted to have three Manhattans along with his dinner, and Bill kept him company drink by drink. This stretched out the meal; and as our time at the restaurant dragged on, I became restless, wanting to get back to the hospice. I started broadly hinting about leaving as we approached the two-hour mark. The hospice staff had indicated to us that we should finish visiting around 10:00 PM; and at the rate we were going, it was going to be pushing up against 9:30 before we got back there. Finally, as Dad finished the last sip of his third drink, I made a direct plea. "Dad, I'd really like to get over to the hospice. I won't be getting to see Mom tomorrow, and it's getting late."

Edie and Bill had been ready to go for a while. Dad seemed to nod his agreement, and I thought we had a done deal. So, when our waitress came by and asked if anyone wanted dessert, I spoke up.

"No, I think that we'd just like the check."

"Wait a minute," Dad responded loudly. "Nobody is going anywhere until I have a cup of coffee. Please bring me one, Miss."

"Dad! I may not get a chance to talk to Mom again. I want to go."

"You can wait."

I couldn't control my exasperation.

"Dad, come on! This is something that you can do for me. It's very important to me."

"Well, this is something that you can do for me. I want my cup of coffee, and I want to sit here and enjoy it!"

"Forget it! I'm out of here!"

I was furious. I turned around, walked to the exit, and went outside to blow off steam. Gentleman Jim's sits on U.S. Route 1, at a point where there is nothing but a congested strip. So, there wasn't any desirable place to walk. Instead, I parked myself on a bench immediately outside the entrance, and tried to calm down. It wasn't easy. There was a pleasant evening breeze that would normally have been soothing, but I was too upset to enjoy it. Dad and I had our history of getting into arguments after he had a few drinks. They were rarely serious, but always a pain. This was a classic one, and it was particularly absurd. As I saw it, Mom was dying and my final good-bye was getting cut short over an extra cocktail and a damn cup of coffee. I tried to look at it from Dad's point of view, but couldn't see any logical defense. Yet, eventually, fuming alone enabled me to settle down enough to walk back inside to try to patch things up.

As I reached our table, I saw that Dad had skipped the cup of coffee. He was looking over the dinner bill trying to figure out what size tip to leave, and Edie and Bill each gave me a look indicating that they had soothed things over. Soon we were on the road to the hospice; not another word was said about the argument. Although we didn't have much time to visit with Mom, everyone was thoughtful about allowing me the final minutes alone with her. Exhausted, but wearing the satisfied look of someone who has completed a job well done, Mom got right to the point.

"Now, when Diane gets here on Monday, everything will be complete. I'm really looking forward to seeing Diane."

"It won't be long, Mom. She'll be here. It's been great being with you, and I'm really glad that you're here instead of at the hospital."

"It's been good seeing you, Donn. Thanks so much for coming."

"You're always with me, Mom."

"Good."

"Nobody could ever ask for more from a mother. Thanks for everything."

"You're a good son, Donn. I'm so happy that things have gone well for you."

"You know, there were two other times that I thought I was saying good-bye to you for the last time, and I was wrong each time; but I think this might finally be it."

"I know."

"Of course, if you decide that you want to stay alive, that door is always open. Just because we've been talking so much about death doesn't mean that you have to take the option. But if you do get better, I'm going to start calling you Lazarus."

"Back from the dead," she laughed.

"Well, Mom. they're waiting outside. I guess that I'd better go now."

"You know, it's not like it's a cold winter night where they have to sit waiting in the car. It's nice out there. They can wait a little longer!"

So, we talked a bit more, especially reminiscing about the years that Nancy, Lynn and Scott lived with us. And as we spoke, she began to drift off. When it was apparent that she couldn't force herself to stay awake any longer, I asked if she would like to sleep. She nodded, and whispered a quiet, "Yes."

"Okay. Good-bye, Mom. I love you."

I kissed her forehead, and walked out to the car.

Diane and the kids met me at the airport. It was wonderful seeing them, but I was feeling pretty numb. We would only have about eighteen hours together before Diane would be leaving for Florida. We spent a large block of that time at the home of our friends Sylvia and Francis Helfrick, who hosted a garden party featuring a string quartet consisting of members of the Manchester (CT.) Symphony Orchestra. Both Sylvia and Francis were retired physicians who had long been active supporters of the orchestra, for which Sylvia performed the viola. The party was a special event, as Sylvia was in remission from cancer, and Francis had arranged the concert in her honor. Although I was tired and emotionally torn, it was a good place to be, especially since there were many close friends attending who were members of our Quaker Meeting.

Then, in what seemed like no time at all, I was seeing Diane off at the airport. After landing in Ft. Lauderdale, she took a limousine to Mom and Dad's condo, and she and Dad immediately drove over to see Mom, who was awake when they arrived. Mom told Diane how happy she was to see her and how pretty she looked. She also asked questions about all three of the kids and chatted a bit more, before tiring and indicating that she needed to sleep. Diane and Dad said good-bye, indicating that they would be back after dinner. When they returned, Mom was asleep. She never awoke again. Diane spent the entire week supporting Dad and sitting by Mom's unconscious body as she went through the final ravaging stages of uremic poisoning. We were assured that, because of the morphine she was receiving, Mom wasn't in pain; but Diane's descriptions of those last days make it clear that her body was in a wrenching battle to the end. There was much labored breathing and occasional jerking motions. When death finally came, the following Saturday, Diane and Dad weren't present, having left to get something to eat. It wasn't the sort of peaceful transition surrounded by family that we had hoped for; but for me there was satisfying closure, as I've always focused on what Mom said to me during my final visit with her:

"Now when Diane gets here on Monday, everything will be complete."

Diane and Dad picked out a casket, and flew up to Philadelphia in the same plane as Mom's body. We only planned a small graveside service, and I was worried because the forecast was for heavy thunder showers. But the storm front passed through earlier than expected, giving way to a warm, breezy, beautiful day.

Though few people outside of the immediate family attended, Diane's family all came and several of Mom and Dad's old friends from the Philadelphia area also managed to make it. Dad, wearing a suit that I helped him pick out the day before, seemed to be operating on automatic pilot. Jenny, almost six and too young to be too distressed by what was happening, held up well through it all. But Philip, nearly ten, was a wreck. After the ceremony, I spent a lot of time walking with him and hugging him as he cried. Soon, almost everyone departed to Edie and Bill's for a picnic meal.

Left alone, Diane, the kids and I stood by Mom's grave. All morning, David, approaching fourteen, had shown less emotion than I had expected; but I reminded myself that he was anxious to be recognized as someone nearly grown up. So, it seemed understandable. I pulled out my harmonica and played *Amazing Grace*. We all turned and walked towards our parked car; but out of the corner of my eye, I spotted David slipping away from the rest of us. Thinking that he was going unnoticed, he bent over and gently kissed Mom's burial marker.

9

FINAL JOURNEY

A little over eight months later, I was flying to Florida to visit my hospitalized father. My flight arrived in Orlando at 12:30 P.M. After quickly eating some lunch at the airport, I grabbed a taxi that dropped me off at Central Regional Hospital in Sanford around 2:15. Identifying myself at the hospital information desk, I inquired about Dad's room, and was informed that he was in number 339. Then, while turning to walk to the elevator, I came face-to-face with a large, gentle-looking man who appeared to be of Asian-Indian descent.

"Did I hear you say that you are Mr. Weinholtz?"

"Yes, are you Dr. Tagore?

"Yes, sir. It is a pleasure to meet you."

"Likewise. How's my father doing?"

"Your father now appears not only to have stabilized, but also to have made some progress. I have just requested that some figures be faxed to me from his physician in Stuart to establish a baseline and to determine if there is some renal involvement. But there is now reason for hope; whereas when we spoke yesterday, it appeared that he wouldn't live much longer."

"That's great. It's hard to keep the old guy down. Can I go see him right away?"

"Of course. I'll join you."

Arriving with no firm notion of Dr. Tagore's clinical ability, I trusted him immediately. Based on our previous phone conversations, it was clear that he was an exceptionally good listener. Now seeing him, his entire manner communicated compassion and competence. Many years in medical education had taught me that this was no guarantee of actual problem-solving ability, but to me communication skills and empathy are so important that I was won over, until events might convince me otherwise.

As I walked into his room, Dad, looking weak and disheveled in a hospital gown with messed-up hair and oxygen tubes inserted in his nose, beamed me a look of excitement and relief. I walked over to the side of his bed, and he reached for my hands, which he held tightly as he stared at me through misty eyes. We didn't say anything for a while, then I spoke.

"You still have that good, strong grip!"

"Did you figure that something was wrong when I didn't show up? How did you find me? Did they call you from the hospital?"

"Well, Dad, it was a little more complicated than that, but I'm here now. And we'll have someone here with you until you get home to Vista Del Lago."

I only stayed a short time, then caught another cab to the Marina Hotel, checked-in, called Diane, picked up Dad's car, and grabbed a quick bite to eat at a nearby McDonald's. Then, I returned to sit by Dad's bed and watch a 49er's-Cowboys play-off game. Throughout the game, Dad spoke very little, but he watched with obvious interest, causing me to feel somewhat encouraged about his alertness and prospects for recovery. Our routine remained very similar over the next three days. Each morning, I'd leave my motel room, go running three or four miles, shower, catch breakfast at McDonald's; then sit by Dad's bed chatting, watching TV or doing work that I had brought with me. I'd only leave for lunch and dinner, or to make phone calls to Diane, Bill or other family members; and would return to the motel from the hospital around 10:00 P.M. each night. For his part, Dad showed some modest improvement. On Tuesday, he was no longer using the oxygen mask. By Wednesday, he was sitting up in a chair for about an hour, and Dr. Tagore and I began talking about what steps to take following Dad's likely discharge, perhaps at the end of the following week. He put me in touch with a hospital social worker, who discussed with me the types of intermediate care facilities that I should be investigating in the Sanford area, as well as in Stuart; since it was clear that Dad was not going to be in a position to immediately return home and care for himself, even with help of visiting nurses. Taking things a step further, Diane and I began talking about similar facilities near us in Connecticut, and about the possibility of remodeling our house so Dad could live with us over the long-term.

Expecting this last idea to be a tough sell with Dad, on Wednesday afternoon I tried raising the issue, so he would have some time to get used to the idea. At the time, Dad was ignoring the rest of his lunch and devouring a large piece of apple pie; a good sign as it was the most interest he had shown in food since my arrival. While he ate, I probed.

"So, Dad, what are your goals here?"

"What do you mean?"

"Well, what are you thinking about trying to accomplish given this whole situation you're in. Do you want to get back to being on your own at Vista Del Lago? Would you like to look into an assisted living situation? Or would you like to come live with Diane, the kids and me? We'd love to have you, if you want to."

He paused briefly, chewed on his pie, and in a rather spritely and emphatic way, given his condition, responded.

"I'll tell you one thing. I plan to live!"

Recognizing this was his way of telling me that I was getting way ahead of the game, I backed off a bit, but alerted him to the need to return to the topic.

"Okay. I guess that it's a little early to start hitting you with stuff like this; but they are already talking about discharging you at the end of next week, and when it's time to get out of here we're going to have to know where you want to go. So please give it a little thought; and when you're ready, let me know what you think. Alright?"

"Alright."

Dad eagerly returned to his pie, and I went back to doing some work, still worried about the next steps. It was going to be hard to oversee Dad's care from afar, and I dearly wished that he would come to live with us, or with Edie and Bill. Just getting through the next week was going to be difficult enough, as I couldn't take another week away from work, and the timing was also bad for Diane, Edie and Bill. Fortunately, Lynn, who was working part-time and had some flexibility, agreed to come down and spend a week.

Then, if necessary, Bill would fly down to take over. We arranged for Lynn to fly in on Friday morning, with me picking her up at the Orlando airport and getting her situated at the Marina Motel. Then, she would take me to the airport to fly to Connecticut on Saturday morning. About 7:00 on Wednesday evening, I left Dad's room to go to a pay-phone, call Bill with the daily report, and talk over both short and long-term plans. Bill had been encouraged by Dad's improved lab tests; but not being there, he didn't have an accurate gauge on Dad's status. He was hoping that Dad might be able to go right back to Vista Del Lago, but I told him that wasn't feasible for a while, if ever. I was especially concerned that Dad, though clearly showing signs of bouncing back, didn't seem sufficiently alert to care for himself. In particular, although demonstrating some interest in sports on TV, he wasn't reading anything at all. Throughout his retirement Dad had been a voracious reader of historical and spy novels, even after his stroke and Mom's death. His lack of interest in any books, or in even glancing at the newspaper's sports page, had me wondering how optimistic we could be. Still, Dad was trying to fight back from a serious health assault; and, as Bill pointed out, time and rest might prove remarkably helpful.

After hanging up the phone, I walked back to Dad's room pondering how things were going to unfold; but upon entering the room, I was startled out of my wits. Dad was experiencing some sort of attack. He appeared panic stricken, his eyes opened wide and his mouth rapidly puckering, like a fish out of water desperately gasping for oxygen. He was sweating profusely. Having no idea what was actually happening, I thought that Dad might be dying at that very moment. So, I quickly hit the nursing call button; then held his hand, leaned directly over his face, and repeatedly told him how much I loved him.

The nurse who responded to the call applied an oxygen mask, gave Dad liquid Tylenol for fever, and indicated that he should be okay soon. As she was a part-time nurse, who had never seen Dad before, I wasn't confident in her assessment, and insisted that she contact a physician. She reached Dr. Tagore by phone, and I described to him my perceptions of what had occurred. Soon afterwards, the internist on call arrived, examined Dad, and increased the oxygen flow. Unable, or perhaps willing, to explain to me what had happened, he assured me that Dad should be much better by morning, but I remained skeptical.

Although his panic subsided, Dad kept puckering and was unable to speak for almost 3-hours. Finally, around 10:00 PM he drifted off to sleep and the puckering stopped. Finally experiencing some relief of my own, I kissed him on the forehead, made my way back to the motel, and tried to get some sleep; only to fail miserably, tossing and turning throughout the night, worrying constantly about Dad's condition, and haunted by his panicked look and the constant puckering.

The next morning, I was deeply disappointed to find that Dad still could not speak and was again puckering, though still receiving oxygen through nasal tubes. I immediately asked that Dr. Tagore be paged. We talked on the phone, and Dad was again placed on a mask in order to increase the oxygen flow. Later, when Dr. Tagore made his rounds, he was taken aback by Dad's condition, and requested that a pulmonologist visit the room. While we waited in the room for the second physician, Dr. Tagore asked me questions on everything I had observed about Dad's condition from the previous evening before the onset of his attack until the present. Suddenly, he mentioned that Dad might need a feeding tube. Whereupon, uncomfortable with having a frank discussion in front of Dad, who was conscious but not responsive, I asked that we might move to the hallway.

Since my arrival at the hospital the previous Sunday, Dad had repeatedly and vigorously asserted to me that he expected me to protect him from either a respirator or a feeding tube. When we reached the hallway, I reminded Dr. Tagore of our initial conversation, via phone from North Carolina, about Dad's wishes, and informed him of Dad's further insistence about these matters during the last several days. Dr. Tagore assured me that he understood, but pleaded that a short time on a feeding tube might be all that Dad needed to regain his strength, enabling him to win his battle. His argument left me feeling terribly torn, and we agreed to postpone the discussion for another twenty-four hours, seeing how Dad progressed. We returned to Dad's room just as the pulmonologist arrived. He performed an examination and speculated that Dad might have aspirated a piece of food, which I suspected could have been from the remaining portion of apple pie that Dad had saved from lunch. He then scheduled Dad for a chest x-ray later in the day. As the physicians were leaving the room, the telephone rang. I answered, and was pleased to hear that it was Diane on the other end. She asked how Dad was doing, and I explained that he hadn't spoken all morning, but that he might like to hear her voice. I moved the phone towards Dad's head, explaining that Diane would like to talk to him. Then, looking particularly irritated with me, Dad grabbed the phone out of my hand and put it up to his ear. He didn't say anything for the several minutes that Diane chatted with him, but just before handing the phone back to me, he weakly bid Diane farewell, uttering, "I love you too."

I was thrilled to hear Dad speak; but also distressed that he seemed upset with me, and worried about what he had overheard when Dr. Tagore mentioned a feeding tube. Throughout the day I tried engaging him in conversation about what was bothering him; but he never answered me, which only upset me more. The only thing that kept me from getting too down was that when Bill, Edie, and Scott all called that afternoon, Dad listened, but didn't speak to them either.

In the meantime, Dad's lab results, including blood oxygen and creatinine levels, began sliding in negative directions, and his chest x-ray showed indications of pneumonia in the lung that had not been affected when he was originally admitted to the hospital. That evening, after returning to the hospital following dinner, I called Bill from the lobby phone, warning him that things seemed to have taken a turn for the worse. We discussed the likelihood that Dad could have similar setbacks at any given time, and that there was no predicting how long he would be in the hospital, much less how things would eventually be resolved. Bill also pointed out that I had been under tremendous stress for almost a week, and that it was time for the reserves to arrive, giving me a breather. He was right. I was exhausted and emotionally ripped, desperately wanting to be with Diane and the kids, but hating the thought of leaving Dad in the hospital; and especially not wanting to depart Florida with him angry at me.

All of these thoughts were racing through my head as I took the elevator up from the hospital lobby and walked down the hallway to Dad's room. Upon reaching 339, I turned right, entered the doorway, and called to Dad. No sooner were the words, "So, how are you doing?" out of my mouth than I saw that Dad wasn't in his bed. Not only was he gone, there was no sign of any of his belongings, and the bed was freshly made. I panicked.

"Jesus! He died and they didn't even let me know. No! They must have moved him to another part of the hospital. He couldn't possibly have died. But maybe he did, or maybe he had another attack like he did last night. Maybe he's in intensive care. I've got to find out what's going on here."

Then, while running down the hall towards the nursing station, things didn't look quite right. Coming to a screeching halt, I examined the numbers above some of the other rooms. They all started with two's! I wasn't on the third floor at all, but on the second. I had gotten off of the elevator too soon. Sheepishly returning to the room that I had just come from, I confirmed for myself that it was 239 not 339. I felt like a stupid ass, but at least a greatly relieved stupid ass.

I reentered the elevator, went up a floor, found Dad, and settled in to watch TV with him until about 10:00 PM. His overall condition appeared further weakened, and he still seemed frustrated and angry. He didn't speak to me the entire time; but I could handle that. It was just good to be there with him, though I was more aware than ever that somebody else needed to take over, soon.

E arly Friday morning, I drove to Orlando to pick up Lynn at the airport. It was tremendously reassuring seeing her disembark from the plane, knowing that help had arrived. After we kissed hello, she asked about Dad.

"How's Pop Pop?"

"I haven't been in yet this morning. He's not nearly as good as he was earlier in the week, but he was a lot better yesterday than he was Wednesday night. Whatever happened to him then really set him back. It's going to be day–by-day. He may continue getting better, or he may take another downturn. Who knows!"

"Well, we'll perk him up. I brought some soft pretzels from Philadelphia. Put some mustard on them, and wave them in front of him, and he'll be a new man."

"Hey, just what the doctor ordered!"

We drove directly to the hospital, and as soon as we walked into Dad's room, I could sense a difference from the day before. He seemed substantially weaker, but his eyes looked brighter and more content. He had given up his anger. As soon as he saw Lynn, he managed a weak smile; and when she leaned over to kiss him hello, he mouthed, "I love you." Still, he spoke no audible words throughout the morning. When Doctor Tagore stopped in during his rounds, he checked Dad over, then discretely signaled to me that he would like to talk in the hallway.

"As I've told you before, your father has a remarkable constitution, very resilient protoplasm. It is amazing that he has weathered as much as he has and is still alive, especially given his lifetime of smoking and drinking. But now he is losing strength. He has a fighting chance, if we can get him some nourishment, but without some food I am sure that he won't make it. He's now experiencing renal problems following the trauma of Wednesday night, when he experienced the early stages of congestive heart failure probably brought on by a new bout of pneumonia, due to aspirating some food. He responded to lasix. We were able to clear the fluid from his lungs, but too many of his numbers are now headed down."

"Do you think that he might also have had a small stroke?"

I hoped that he would answer affirmatively, because a stroke would help explain Dad's earlier frustration and anger, indicating that he might not have been angry with me after all.

"I don't think so. There isn't any clear focal point that would enable us to conclude that there has been damage to the brain."

"What about his lack of speech? I've only heard him say three words since the episode on Wednesday."

"You're right. That is a focal point. However, the question of whether or not your father had a stoke is of secondary importance right now."

"So, we're back to the feeding tube issue."

"Yes, you've made it very clear to me that your father doesn't wish to have either a feeding tube or a respirator as a prolonged method of life support. He also has told me so himself. I understand, and I am sympathetic. Yet, if we could simply insert a tube for as little as forty-eight hours, we could provide him with the nourishment that his body desperately needs in order to rally to the challenge of this current assault. I promise you that the tube will not be left in to unnecessarily sustain your father's life."

I didn't question Dr. Tagore's judgement or his word. Even though I was momentarily distressed by the fact that he hadn't factored in Dad's speech loss. It was clear to me that he was an honest, compassionate man whose argument made sense. What disturbed me was wondering what Dad would think, given that I had repeatedly guaranteed him that there would be no feeding tube. In his current condition, I didn't think that he'd understand that a tube would only be temporarily inserted. So, I hemmed and hawed, but finally agreed. Whereupon Dr. Tagore assured me that it was the right decision, then reassured me that the tube wouldn't stay in for more than a few days. He would submit the request for the tube later that afternoon, but it might not be inserted until early the following morning. Lynn and I spent the afternoon at the hospital, taking turns sitting and chatting with Dad, even though he didn't speak back. He was very weak, and his laboratory numbers continued slipping in the wrong direction. Still, it seemed plausible that he might rebound once benefiting from some food. At least, he wasn't suffering from the convulsive puckering of Wednesday night and Thursday; and much to my relief, he no longer showed any hint of Thursday's anger.

Around 5:30 PM, Lynn and I kissed Dad good-bye, then went to the Marina Hotel. We got Lynn a room, and while she showered, I went for a run around Sanford. It was already dark, but I enjoyed running through the deserted, though well lit, town streets. While covering my usual three miles, I spotted a seafood grill that looked appealing. So, after I showered, we walked to the grill so we might get a good meal and Lynn could get some exercise of her own. Unfortunately, by the time that we got there the grill was closing, and we had to turn around and walk back to the Marina Hotel's restaurant.

Along the way, we caught up on each other's lives, in particular Lynn's impending engagement to her future husband, Dan; and we discussed the range of options that we might pursue regarding getting Dad out of the hospital and into long-term care. Finishing our meal close to 9:00 PM, we hurried back to the hospital to spend a little time with Dad and wish him a good night.

Entering his room, we were shocked to see that the feeding tube was already in place. We hadn't expected it until morning, and had wanted to prepare him, but it was too late! Furthermore, although Dad was asleep, he looked terrible. His mouth was wide open; his eye's were closed, but not peacefully. I worried that he might not wake up at all. We gently tried to awaken him to assure him that the feeding tube was a temporary measure, but he didn't respond.

I had Dr. Tagore paged. As we talked, he told me that, given Dad's poor afternoon laboratory results, his survival might depend on dialysis.

"Oh, God!" I thought, "I promised him this wasn't going to happen." And I reminded Dr. Tagore about Dad's wishes for no heroic measures.

"I remember," he responded, "but I'd be negligent, if I didn't inform you of what might be necessary."

Then he pointed out that dramatic benefits from the nutrition resulting from the feeding tube might well appear within twenty-four hours.

Assured that no additional, extraordinary steps of any kind would betaken over night, Lynn and I returned to the motel to get some sleep. Lying in bed, I suffered horribly mixed emotions. Though anxious to get home to be with my family, especially since Jenny was getting especially concerned about me being away, I doubted that I could leave the next morning; not with Dad teetering on the brink. After tossing and turning for hours, I eventually got to sleep by convincing myself that the feeding tube would work. After all, this was "Dad," the man of the "resilient protoplasm!" Awaking in the morning, I felt energized with a surprisingly confident sense that my mission was to get home with Diane and the kids, get rested up, and return to Florida when needed. Feeling comfortable leaving things in Lynn's hands, I wanted to quickly get to the airport and head off to Connecticut. But first, we would swing by the hospital, so I could say good-bye to Dad, who surely would be benefiting from the nutrition he was now receiving. I'd tell him that the feeding tube was only temporary, that we would always have at least one family member with him, and that I'd call him daily until I returned to Florida.

That was my plan. But when Lynn and I entered the hospital room, it took one brief look at Dad for me to sigh, "God! There's no way that I can leave today." Rather than improving over night, Dad had deteriorated dramatically. His eyes were open, but rolled upward in an eerie, death-like stare. He showed no visible response to either calls or touch. His nurse informed us that his BUN (blood urea nitrogen) and white blood cell counts had shot way up over night, both ominous signs.

A new pulmonary physician entered the room, introduced himself, and began examining Dad. Lynn and I told him how distressed we were over Dad's downturn; but new to the case, he showed little empathy. He did, however, page Dr. Tagore; and shared with him, over the phone, in medical jargon, his perceptions of Dad's condition. Before he could hang up, I told him that I would like to speak to Dr. Tagore.

"Dr. Tagore!"

"Yes."

"It's not good."

"No, it's not. Your father is in much more serious condition than he's ever been, even worse than when he was first brought into the hospital."

"I realize that. I think that he's going to die soon."

"That's quite possible, but he may linger for several days. It's hard to tell."

At that exact moment, convinced that his struggle for survival was over, I fixated on a single goal. It was time for Dad to go home, and I was going to get him there.

"Under these circumstances, I'd like to have the feeding tube removed and have my father discharged to hospice care."

"Are you sure that's what you want?"

"Yes. My father doesn't want to continue on like this. He made that clear to me and to you. He's in a far weaker state than my mother was when she made a similar decision. It's time."

"I think you are right. Now is perhaps the proper time for hospice care. But where will you have him placed? I doubt that the local hospice will have any beds available."

"I want to take him to the Hospice of Martin. They probably won't have any beds either, but I'm sure that they'll admit him for home hospice care. I've dealt with them before. They're wonderfully supportive."

"You're looking at an ambulance ride of almost three hours. Your father may not survive the trip."

"I'm willing to take that risk."

"I'll be coming to the hospital in about two hours. I must examine your father again to determine if there has been any improvement. If not, I'll sign the discharge papers."

"That will give me time to contact my brother and my wife, to make sure that they're comfortable with this; and to work things out with the hospice."

"You'll also have to get in touch with an ambulance company. Some may not be willing to transport a patient this sick such a distance."

"How can I find out who to call?"

"The Social Work Department will be able to help you."

"Thank you Dr. Tagore, I'll see you in a few hours."

"Good luck."

There was no time to waste. Everything was going to have to unfold perfectly to get Dad home that afternoon. I moved into high gear, informing Lynn what was going to happen, rather than consulting with her. I knew this was harsh; but I was on a crusade. Come hell or high water, I wasn't going to let Dad die in a strange hospital over a hundred and fifty miles from his home. He had assured me that he could make it to Philadelphia for Christmas, then get back to Stuart. I was going to make sure that he completed his trip.

After calling US Air to cancel my tickets, I phoned Diane. It was very comforting to talk to her, and she was supportive of the hospice plan. Then I contacted Edie and Bill, who were in New York City with a group of friends. Bill was shocked that Dad had taken such a turn for the worse, but he told me that he trusted my judgement.

"After all, Donn, you're the one who's there; and you know how good I feel about the people at the hospice."

"Thanks, Bill. I really think that this is what we have to do, even though there is a chance that Dad might not survive the trip."

"If anyone can make it, he will. Should I come down right away."

"I don't think so. Finish your weekend in New York, and fly down on Sunday night or Monday. You couldn't get down here until late tonight anyway. Let Lynn and me get things set up."

"Okay, keep me posted. Edie and I will check into what flights are available. We'll drive home early tomorrow morning, and probably catch an afternoon flight out of Philly. Thanks for doing all of this, Donn. I love you, Brother"

"I love you too, Bill. See you soon."

Reassured, I called the Hospice of Martin. As expected, no beds were available, but they were open to providing home hospice care. In fact, they promised to have a nurse and a hospital bed waiting for us when we got to Dad's apartment. We only had to fax them the appropriate paperwork, and have someone let them into the apartment beforehand. So, I called Aunt Ruth and arranged for her to meet the nurse and the bed deliveryman. Then, I called the hospice back, asking them to fax the forms for me and Dr. Tagore to sign. Next, I alerted the hospital social worker and the nurses that Dad was going to be discharged. The social worker gave me the names of local ambulance companies.

The first ambulance service I called was willing to transport Dad to Stuart, but their representative warned me that it would cost over a thousand dollars, which wouldn't be covered by Medicare. I assured her that the cost wasn't a problem, and we made arrangements for the ambulance crew to meet Lynn and me around 1:30 PM. Meanwhile Lynn, who had been sitting with Dad throughout, picked up the papers faxed by the hospice, brought them to me, and went across town to check out of the motel. I filled out what I could prior to Dr. Tagore's arrival.

He appeared, a little after 1:00 PM. Dad hadn't improved, and after a brief physical examination, Dr. Tagore signed the papers discharging Dad into hospice care. Afterward, we stood in the hallway, and he confided to me.

"I think that you are doing a good thing. Your father will die quietly at home. He may never be conscious of it, but you and your family will have greater peace."

"And he'll have completed his trip!"

"Yes, he'll have completed his trip."

By then I was obsessed with the notion of finishing "the trip." Realistically, I had no idea how important it might have been to Dad, if he were conscious, to get back to Stuart, but I convinced myself that it must be. Completing the trip would be our final accomplishment together. In a poetic culmination to Dad's life, with time running out on the clock, we would metaphorically push the ball over the goal line for Dad's final victory. Fate had delivered the challenge. We were going for it!

While we were still standing in the hallway, two emergency medical technicians from the ambulance service arrived. Both were women. Jackie was the more experienced and more vocal of the two. Kathy kept a lower profile, deferring to her partner on all decisions. After introducing herself, Jackie explained that the trip would take approximately three hours, and she sought confirmation from Dr. Tagore that we'd be received by hospice representatives. After getting this assurance, we all walked into Dad's room; where upon, after taking one look at Dad, Jackie immediately became visibly distressed. She turned to me.

"Mr. Weinholtz, I'm afraid I didn't realize just how serious a condition your father's in. If he goes into arrest anywhere during the trip, I'm required by state law to begin emergency resuscitation procedures and go immediately to the nearest hospital, where they will also try to revive him."

"But that's crazy! We are taking him home to die, not to be resuscitated. He's already been discharged into hospice care!"

"I realize that, Sir; but the problem is that we're transporting him across county lines. Once I'm out of my home county, I have to follow the protocols set by the state. I've got no choice."

"God. That's awful. That's the last thing in the world that he'd want."

"I know, Sir. Let me call my supervisor, to see if I have any other options. But I think the only other alternative is to use the helicopter, and that would be very expensive."

As much as I wanted to get Dad home, the helicopter was not

an option. It wasn't the expense, which I knew would come out of Dad's estate. It was the absurdity of the idea. Why pull out of commission an emergency vehicle, that might be needed to save a life, in order to transport someone home to die! A helicopter seemed too precious a commodity to use capriciously. No, we'd make a go of it by ambulance. I was sure that Dad was destined to make it home. He'd survive the journey, no matter how close to death he appeared. But we couldn't waste any more time. So, when Lynn suggested that maybe we should call Diane and Bill to see what they thought about how to transport Dad, I quickly responded.

"No, we're going to go by ambulance. You can drive Dad's car. I'll ride with him. We've got to get going, fast!"

Meanwhile, out of the corner of my eye, I spotted Jackie, in the hallway talking to her supervisor on a portable, two-way radio, explaining the situation and checking into the helicopter possibility. Unaware that I could hear her, she exclaimed,

"There's no way this man is going to make it!"

And I thought to myself, "No, he's going to make it. We just have to get our asses on the road!"

Jackie got off of the radio, and began explaining to me the steps necessary to secure the helicopter. Hearing that I had ruled out that option, she looked increasingly nervous and reiterated the procedures she would have to follow if Dad went into cardiac arrest along the way. I told her that I understood, and was willing to take the risk.

"Okay, let's get to it," she said, biting her lip, but clearly communicating that she was willing to move into action once a decision was made.

While Jackie and Kathy began preparing Dad for transfer to the ambulance, I made two quick telephone calls; one to Aunt Ruth to ask her to open the apartment for the hospice nurse, the other to the hospice to confirm that everything was moving forward as planned. Then, Lynn and I said our good-byes to the nurses and other hospital personnel who had been so helpful, including Dr. Tagore, a model of patience and kindness. I put in a hurried call to Diane telling her that we were on our way, and asked her to phone Edie and Bill to alert them. Within minutes, we were standing in the bright Florida sunlight, sliding Dad's stretcher bed into the ambulance. Then, Jackie hooked Dad up to supplemental oxygen and some sort of monitor. Meanwhile, I leaned over him, whispering different variations of, "We're going home to Vista, Dad. You're going to finish your trip." Suddenly, we were off, Kathy driving the ambulance, Jackie and me in the back, and Lynn following close behind in Dad's car.

Given the morning's craziness, I entered the ambulance hoping for three hours of peaceful, reflective time with Dad. When we started driving, even though there was absolutely no indication that he was hearing me, I held Dad's hand, quietly and repeatedly telling him that he would soon be home. But within minutes, it became clear that Jackie, a self-described "adrenaline junkie," was extraordinarily nervous; maybe because she wasn't practicing her typical rescue behaviors, maybe because she was worried about me. Whatever the reason, she began talking to me soon after we left the hospital. Initially, she explained to me how strange it was for her to simply sit there because she was used to the high drama of trying to save a life. After we had cycled through this issue a few times, she began asking questions about Dad, then about Mom and their relationship, and then about Diane, me and our marriage. At first, I gave short answers, trying to send the message that I wanted some quiet. But I never broke through to Jackie, and I started feeling irritated and frustrated over the bizarre circumstances that were unfolding.

Yet, the more that I listened to Jackie, the more apparent it became that she was a good-hearted soul. So, I submitted, somewhat, and shared more information with her. This, in turn, led Jackie to disclose a remarkable amount of detail about her personal life, including the conditions that had led to her splitting with her former live-in boyfriend, who she believed she still loved very much. Jackie had felt stifled by the closeness of the committed relationship that he so desired. Consequently, she left New York, where she had always lived, for Florida, where she had been for the last couple of years. In spite of their separation, she maintained a long-distance relationship with the boyfriend, and he remained remarkably supportive of her.

Somewhere along the line, as Jackie's lengthy story unfolded, I completely let go of the notion that I could meaningfully communicate with Dad, either verbally or telepathically. Instead, I chose to be contented with holding his hand and quietly listening to Jackie, occasionally offering insights about solid relationships like Mom's and Dad's and Diane's and mine. It felt odd because the circumstances were so much different, indeed comically different, than what I had expected; but it was a good lesson about the fact that life doesn't allow us to perfectly script our own melodramas. For this particular three hours, destiny, if there is any such thing, reserved time for Jackie and me to be talking to each other.

We reached Stuart around 6:00 PM and proceeded directly to Vista Del Lago. The sun had set, and we were greeted by a calm, windless dusk as we pulled into the parking lot next to Dad's apartment building. Aunt Ruth and the hospice nurse, Sally, were waiting for us; and a hospital bed was ready for Dad in the den, the exact same location that Mom had occupied the previous May. The next challenge was transporting Dad up the narrow winding stairwell to the second floor. It was a tight squeeze, but Jackie, Kathy, Lynn and I were able to negotiate the turns, and soon Dad was resting peacefully in the hospital bed.

I felt incredibly relieved, and whispered in his ear.

"You're home, Dad. You're home in Stuart. You're in your den. I knew you could do it!"

I kissed him on the forehead, and headed outside to help Jackie take the stretcher to the ambulance. When we reached the bottom of the stairs, I gave Jackie and Kathy some money, above the cost of the ambulance charge, for all the trouble that they had been through. Both adamantly resisted taking it, but when I insisted that Dad would have it no other way, they relented. We were in the process of saying goodbye, when suddenly Lynn appeared at the top of the stairs crying.

"Donn! Donn! Come quick. I think PopPop is dying."

I sprinted up the stairs into the apartment and back to the den. Reaching Dad, who was breathing deep, loud, intermittent breaths, as though moaning in rhythmic waves, I blurted out, "Dad! I love you!" Then, abruptly, with one last sigh, he stopped. The sudden shift to silence was the most heart-wrenching moment of my life. It was as though Dad's soul had suddenly lurched free of his body, profoundly proclaiming that he was gone.[1]

I stood next to Dad's lifeless body, feeling totally alone, crushed by the loss. I hugged him and I cried; but within minutes, felt an overwhelming need to press on. Soon, Sally examined Dad, declared him dead, and called the information into the hospice. I bid farewell to Jackie and Kathy, then called Aycock's Funeral Home, to request that someone come to pick up Dad's body. While talking to their representative, I also scheduled a meeting for the following afternoon, so Lynn and I could select a casket and make arrangements for sending Dad to Philadelphia. Next, I called Diane and the kids. Finally, I contacted Edie and Bill.

They were still in New York, and Bill was devastated by the news. He sobbed loudly for a long time. I felt badly for him, but I

---

[1]. I later learned, from reading Sherwin Nuland's How We Die, that Dad was probably dead by the time that I reached him, and that what I most likely witnessed was his body convulsing through the "death rattle," the sounds generated from spasms in the voice box evoked by the increased blood acidity of the newly deceased.

was so pumped up on adrenaline that I couldn't slow down to stay in touch with anyone else's feelings. After I hung up, Lynn made it clear that she was ready to just grieve and call it a day. She pointed out, as the hearse from the funeral home arrived, that we hadn't been able to select clothing for Dad to be buried in, but that we could do so on Sunday morning.

"Let's just call it quits, pick up Aunt Ruth, and go have dinner. I've had it for today!"

No sooner were the words out of her mouth than I shot back:

"No, I'll take care of the clothes now. I know exactly what he should wear, the suit that we picked out for Mom's funeral."

"But, Donn, can't it wait? They're already here. Let's just sit down, catch our breath for a moment, then get something to eat!"

"Lynn. I'm in 'the zone.' I've got to get as much done now as I can. I'm not going to hold us up. I know right where the suit is, and what shirt, tie and shoes to get. It's as good as done."

Marching into Dad's bedroom, I went to his closet and pulled out everything that was needed just as the two men from Aycock's were arriving at our door. Sally, who was a soothing presence and with whom I'd been having a running conversation ever since we had arrived in the ambulance, seemed amused. She had overheard my "in the zone" comment, and was puzzled by the remark.

"What exactly did you mean by 'in the zone'?"

"It's a phrase athletes use to describe those rare times when a game is in perfect focus. You know exactly what you have to do, and you can do it almost effortlessly. That's the way I've felt most of today."

"How so?"

"Well, the last week was really awful; but although I'm having a hard time now, I'm at peace. This morning, when it was clear that Dad was going to die, I knew what I had to do. I had to make sure that Dad completed his trip. Now, I have to make sure that he gets back up to Philadelphia. Then my brother, Bill, can take over."

How this fit into Sally's constellation of hospice memories, I never learned; but she nodded approvingly, and smiled in a way that conveyed that she understood.

After the hearse took Dad away, Lynn, Aunt Ruth and I thanked Sally, said goodbye, and went out for a late supper at the nearby Olive Garden. Since Dad was a regular customer, we assumed the waitresses would be wondering why he hadn't returned after Christmas. After we told our waitress the bad news, a parade of employees came by all telling us how much they were going to miss "Bill." For hours, Lynn, Aunt Ruth and I reminisced about Dad, Mom and Nancy. Even though I rarely drink, I had two large, Margaritas in Dad's memory. For the first time all day, I felt tired and ready to go to sleep.

However, a couple of hours later I was tossing and turning on the sofa bed in Mom and Dad's living room, unable to sleep and beginning to feel ill. By 5:00AM, the torment escalated to a splitting headache and serious nausea. I repeatedly got up to go to the bathroom, disturbing Lynn, who had been sleeping in Mom and Dad's room located across the hallway. About 8:30 or 9:00 AM, Lynn, who teased me about being a poor drinker, went out to buy some breakfast food. Meanwhile, in spite of my upset stomach, I downed several Anacin and drank some tea, for the caffeine, in the hope of breaking the headache.

Soon after Lynn left, it hit me. Feeling unimaginably sad, I began crying in frighteningly deep, wails. Fixated on Nancy, Mom and Dad all being gone, I hurt more than I ever had before. I was completely out of control. It was as though my body was involuntarily purging itself of years of pain. I momentarily gained control, but then it began all over again. There was another lull, but yet another wave of grief. Finally, exhausted, I fell asleep, awakening momentarily when Lynn returned, then falling back into an even deeper sleep.

When I finally awoke, my headache had broken and my stomach, though still queasy, was substantially better. I got up, wandered around the apartment, and even looked for a bite to eat. Lynn asked how I was doing, and I told her about my "breakdown" while she was gone. Soon afterwards, Diane called, then Bill, who emphasized that stress and grief, not the Margaritas, had made me ill. I figured that he was probably right, but that the Margaritas lit the fuse allowing the emotional bomb to explode. About 2:00PM, Lynn and I went to the funeral parlor, picked out a casket, wrote an obituary, and made arrangements to send Dad's body to Philadelphia. After finishing there, we drove to the beach to spend a little time by the ocean before returning to Vista Del Lago for supper at Aunt Ruth's. By evening, I felt completely recovered.

On Monday morning, prior to the 10:30 arrival of the limousine that would take us to the airport, I ran out to the post office to make copies of Dad's will for Lynn, Scott and me. Bill, the executor, was to get the original; but upon returning to the apartment, I discovered that the original will was missing. I couldn't believe it! Bemused but panic stricken, I hopped into the car and headed back to the post office, hoping that I had left it there. While en route, the drawbridge across the St. Lucie River raised for what seemed like an eternity as a slow-moving sailboat passed through. Finally reaching the post office, I ran inside, flipped open the top of the copier and breathed a huge sigh of relief. The will was still there! With the unbelievably careless error corrected, it was finally okay to head home.

On a cold, sunny, winter day, virtually the same group of family and friends gathered for Dad's graveside funeral as had collected for Mom's, months earlier. Once again, the ceremony was short. Dad was laid to rest next to Mom. Edie and Bill had selected the tombstone inscription:

William F. Weinholtz ~ **Agathe Larson Weinholtz**

Feb. 6. 1914–Jan. 21, 1995 ~ Aug. 13, 1914—May 28, 1994

Together Forever

Gada and William, 1989 (Mom's 75th Birthday Party)

10

AFTERSHOCKS

A few weeks after Dad's funeral, Bill and I flew to Florida for a weekend to meet with a lawyer about executing Dad's will. David joined us because I had previously promised a trip to Florida to visit "Pop-Pop." Things went smoothly with the lawyer, and we had a good time taking Aunt Ruth out to dinner, but David never got to enjoy the beach the way that I hoped he would. A major snowstorm was raging in the Northeast and the associated cold front was so strong that Florida received gale winds along with daytime high temperatures in the fifties. We drove to nearby Jensen Beach to survey the windswept sand and incredibly rough ocean. David got to run around on the beach and get his feet wet, but was severely disappointed that he couldn't go swimming. Watching him, I thought, "Poor guy. No PopPop. No swimming. No fun for you."

Phil, Bill, Dave, Edie and Jenny, Tennessee, 1989

By then, Edie and Bill had decided that they would like to keep Mom and Dad's condominium, buying out Lynn's, Scott's and my shares. They planned to retire to Vista Del Lago themselves, liking the idea of carrying on in Mom and Dad's tradition. In April, Diane flew down with Edie, Bill and Lynn to clean out the apartment and make arrangements for shipping some furniture north. Enough time was scheduled to leisurely sort through pictures and Mom's knickknacks, as well as to go out each night for dinner. Diane worked in her morning runs around the condominium complex, along with daily swims in the pool. Bill got out to play some golf. The trip had a healing effect for all, even me. Although I wasn't there, I called each evening to hear how things had gone during the day; and I was pleased that Diane was with my family. Things might finally have been starting to look up, if not for some troubling concerns about Edie's health.

Edie's mother had died several years earlier from uterine cancer; and following our Mom's death, Edie became aware of benign fibroid tumors in her uterus. Over Dad's final Christmas visit, she and Bill, without telling anyone, wrestled with the issue of whether or not Edie should have a hysterectomy for precautionary reasons. Soon after Dad's death, the warning signals of potential future problems became sufficiently clear that Edie opted for the hysterectomy. In February, she entered the hospital for the operation. Following the surgery, immediate indications were that everything was fine; but within days, Edie noticed that she was slurring some words when she spoke. The question haunting us all was, "Why?"

For months, in spite of repeated testing, there was no definitive answer. Then one day, when I was home alone, the phone rang. It was Edie, sounding very cheery.

"Hi, Donn. Guess What!"

"What, Edie?"

"My neurologist knows what I have!"

"Finally! What's the diagnosis?"

"He says that I have pseudobulbar palsy. Do you know what it is?"

"Nope. Never heard of it. What is it?"

"Well, I don't know either. He didn't tell me. He just said that he has pretty conclusive evidence that I have pseudobulbar palsy, and that the symptoms can vary dramatically from patient to patient. Then he let me go without saying much of anything else. So, I decided to call you, figuring that you would know. I guess it can't be too bad, if it is something pseudo!"

Once again, my medical education experience was coming back to haunt me. Painfully aware that my understanding of physician teaching practices translated into little valuable medical knowledge, I squirmed each time a family member asked me a question about a specific illness. It had happened frequently enough that I had learned to confess ignorance up front, do some research, then get back later with an answer. This time, however, Edie was so anxious to hear something that, if possible, I wanted to help her out right away.

"Hold on. Let me see if I can find my *Merck Manual*." I rushed downstairs to our living room bookcase and pulled out our 20 year old copy of the classic diagnosis and therapy desk reference. Turning to the index, I was pleased at quickly being able to find pseudobulbar palsy; and returning to the phone with Edie, flipped to the correct page. "Here it is, page 1353! Let me read for a few seconds, and try to figure this out."

The first thing that caught my eye while scanning the page was the chapter title at the top: *Muscular Atrophies, Dystrophies and Related Disorders*. Then I noticed a heading for progressive bulbar palsy.

"Edie, there is something here about progressive bulbar palsy. It says,*Involvement of the motor nuclei of the medulla makes chewing, swallow-ing and talking difficult. Frequently, involuntary outbursts of laughing and crying occur. Atrophy and fibrillations of the tongue are usual.'"

"That sounds a lot like me. What else does it say?"

Edie seemed so pleased at getting some accurate information that I eagerly pushed on. Noticing a bold reference to pseudobulbar palsy in the page's first paragraph, I quickly scanned backwards.

"It mentions pseudopulbar palsy up above, and it says: 'For some months weakness and spasticity may predominate with little evidence of atrophy. The spasticity may involve the bulbar muscles.' That doesn't tell me too much. I've got to read the previous page."

"Okay, I've waited this long. I can wait a little longer!"

As my eyes darted to page 1352, I was thunderstruck by the section heading staring back at me: *Amytropic Lateral Sclerosis; Progressive (Spinal) Muscular Atrophy: Progressive Bulbar Palsy.* Seeing Amytropic LateralSclerosis (ALS), I immediately began praying that Edie's condition wasn't related to the deadly "Lou Gehrig's Disease." Knowing about ALS's horrendous, irreversible effects; progressive nerve and muscle destruction, eventually rendering the mentally alert patient unable to breathe; I desperately wanted to see that pseudobulbar palsy was something more benign. But my heart sank while silently reading the paragraph that followed: *The three names above represent descriptive subdivisions of one disease. The etiology is unknown; the disease usually occurs after age 40 and more frequently in men. Though some patients have lived beyond 5yr, the prognosis is grave and death usually occurs in 2 to 5 yrs.*"

I panicked as Edie pressed for my findings. Although having prided myself on being able to talk candidly to dying people, I was caught totally off guard, and didn't have a clue what to say.

"Well, what's the verdict, Donn?"

"Edie, it...uh...says that it's...uh...a form of ALS."

"What's ALS?"

"Amy tropic Lateral Sclerosis."

"Which is?"

"Have you ever heard of Lou Gehrig's disease?"

"No."

"Well, it involves progressive nerve and muscle degeneration, and back when this Merck Manual was written the prognosis wasn't very good, but that was almost twenty years ago. I imagine that by now they must be able to do a lot more."

"So how bad was the prognosis back then?"

Edie's tone had changed, her concern now apparent. Feeling shattered, my mind was racing in circles searching for comforting words, while clinging to the slim hope that the latest ALS research and treatments had something to offer. I remained silent for an awkward period. Edie pushed to the bottom line.

"Donn, what was the prognosis back then?"

I hedged, while trying to remain truthful.

"Edie, many people didn't survive beyond five years. But, like I said, this is an old Merck Manual. The potential for new cures is probably pretty great. Look at all they've done with so many other diseases."

"Yeah, you may be right. I hope you're right."

The wind was completely gone from Edie's sails, and from mine. Before saying goodbye, I urged her to return to her doctor to press for more up-to-date information. Then, I told her I loved her, hung up the phone and cried.

I can't begin to do justice to Edie and Bill's story, and will not try. Although we regularly phoned and visited several times a year, my family and I didn't have the day-to-day contact necessary to fully experience the heartache of Edie's slow, relentless, ALS-induced, deterioration. Yet, during our visits we were inspired by the heroism and honesty that Edie, Bill, and their children displayed throughout. Certainly, to some extent our extended family's prior losses prepared them to deal valiantly and sensitively with Edie's fate. But ALS also imposed its own special dynamics. The very nature of the disease prohibits denial, causing people to dig deeply and draw upon their very best. Furthermore, the organized ALS community provides remarkable assistance via education, counseling and structured opportunities for patients and their families within regions to interact and inspire each other. Buoyed by these supports, Edie's spirit was never broken, though her body was defeated. Throughout her life Edie possessed a glowing smile. And somehow, even when the only way that she could communicate was by painstakingly tapping away at a computer, she managed to maintain that glow. Those of us who knew and loved her will always carry her smile with us.

Blessedly, Edie and Bill had many frank discussions about Bill's life after Edie's impending death. Edie made it very clear that she wanted him to marry again, that she knew he would find somebody, but he shouldn't settle for just anybody. After Edie died, Bill met and married Susan. He found life after death.

"Did Dad ever tell you that he was married before he married Mom?"

"WHAT!"

"Did Dad ever tell you that he was married to someone before he married Mom?"

"Cut it out, Bill. Who are you trying to kid?"

"He was. He told me so when Penny and I were getting divorced. He said, *'Bill, I know how things can go wrong. I got divorced once myself.'* Then he told me how after Mom married Bill Smith, he met someone else. It didn't work out, so he got out of it. She moved up to Altoona or somewhere, and the divorce papers are filed up there."

That's how Bill broke it to me. It was a few weeks after Dad died, and I'm not sure what possessed him to tell me at that particular moment; but it was the most bizarre "news" that I had ever experienced, a secret about which no one had ever hinted.

It wasn't such a shock that Dad had never let it slip, as it was always clear that Mom was the only real love of his life. Knowing Dad, I figured that he had probably convinced himself that he was never "truly married" that first time. But it was Mom who surprised me. After all, she had told me about Dad's false teeth, my grandfather's suicide and, over the years, many other juicy tidbits. How could she have kept this one hidden? I told myself that she must have promised Dad not to say anything. Still, I never dreamed that something so significant could have completely eluded me. My ignorance of my own family history was humbling.

Aunt Mary and Uncle Tick, 1982

"Please, no thank you! Please, no thank you!"

The oddly phrased plea came from Aunt Mary, lying in her infirmary bed at the extended care retirement community to which she had moved several years earlier. She wanted nothing to do with the meal Diane and I were urging her to eat.

"Come on, Aunt Mary. You've got to eat something. How about a little Jello?"

"Please, no thank you!"

"Just a little something. I'll feed it to you."

"Maybe some Jello, but nothing else. I'm not hungry right now. Just leave it, and I'll eat the rest after you leave."

"OK. You win."

And she did. Over the course of many months, Aunt Mary, at age seventy, achieved her goal. She systematically starved herself to death. Her intentions weren't clear until the very end, the circumstances unfolded slowly. I was surprised how well Aunt Mary fared following the death of her husband John, better known as *Uncle Tick*, from cancer in 1986. Having no children, Mary and Tick were especially devoted to each other; and Aunt Mary was initially quite sad once Tick, a huge and wonderfully amiable man, was gone. But with a lot of support from her friends and our family in the Philadelphia area, Aunt Mary popped through her depression and, with her friends, began traveling all over the world. She still clearly missed Tick, but she was making a good run at life.

Then, sometime soon after Edie was diagnosed with ALS, Aunt Mary suffered a stroke and was hospitalized. The good news was that she was expected to recover reasonably well, but she would have to spend some time in a rehabilitation facility before returning to her apartment. I started calling her about twice a week, during her rehabilitation, to say, 'Hi!' and to check on her. She sounded as though she was coming along pretty well; but then, during a therapy session, she fell and sustained several injuries that caused her continuous pain. Afterwards, she was never the same. Her desire to live slipped away.

Looking back, I think that, once it became apparent to Aunt Mary that she couldn't easily and fully recover from her fall, she probably assumed that she would be an invalid for the rest of her life. With Uncle Tick, Mom and Nancy gone (and with Edie dying) this was likely too much for her to bear. With dark humor, she and Edie, whose ALS was steadily progressing, used to claim that they would both have to contact Dr. Kevorkian to help them out. Such comments were few and far between, and it was easy to laugh them off. But one day when Diane, the kids and I were visiting her at the rehabilitation center, Aunt Mary tipped her hand, although I didn't realize it at the time. Though obviously deeply frustrated at being bed-ridden, she still managed to joke around quite a bit, which I took as a good sign. However on this particular day, with Diane and the kids out of the room, Aunt Mary grew more serious, expressing her deep concern about Edie and about the killing pace that Bill was maintaining working and caring for Edie, while also frequently running over to see her at the rehabilitation center. Then, looking confident, she said, "But I know what I'm doing. I'm taking matters into my own hands."

At the time, I wasn't sure what she was alluding to, and direct questions yielded only cryptic responses. She seemed so focused that I chose to view her comments as an indication that she was headed in a positive direction. When she was subsequently discharged back to the infirmary of her extended care community, it looked like another good sign. After all, Bill and Edie lived only a few miles away, and she had good friends right there in the complex with her. But the move, her continued joking, and her ample girth, all disguised the fact that she was resolutely embarking on a slow march towards death.

Since we only got down to Philadelphia a couple of times a year, and were so tuned-in on Edie's condition, most of my conversations with Aunt Mary were by phone. She had enough excess weight to draw upon that, whenever we saw her, she looked pretty good. But the last time that we visited was a few months before she died. Although she drank clear fluids, and conceded to a few tiny mouthfuls of food; the more we suggested she eat, the more she plaintively wailed.

"Please, no thank you! Please, no thank you!"

Her intentions were clear.

Uncle Milt and Donn, 1985

Sadly, Dad's sister, Aunt Betty, also suffered a stroke soon after Dad's funeral. She never returned home. While hospitalized, her condition evolved into Alzheimer's, and she no longer recognized anyone. Yet her husband, Uncle Milt, drove to see her nearly every day, until her death. Milt was amazingly fit and remarkably sharp in spite of a small, recent stroke of his own. He lived alone, functioning quite well for a few years after Betty's death. We talked by phone now and then, and I tried to see him whenever we were in the Philadelphia area. The visits were fun, and our kids enjoyed hearing the stories about the wild animals (raccoons, skunks etc) that he fed at night behind his tidy suburban ranch house. Milt remained upbeat, but was very much aware that he was the last of his generation. He eventually sold his home, moved into a nursing care facility and died soon afterward.

Scott & Maryanne (during 1st visit at Susan & Bill's) March, 1999

Nothing could have prepared me for Bill's call in March of 1999.

"Hello, Brother!"

"Hey, Bill. How you doing?"

"OK, but hold onto your hat. You're never going to believe this one."

"Oh, God! I'm not up for any surprises. What is it?"

"I'll give you a hint. You have a relative that you didn't know anything about."

"Yikes! Dad had a kid before me!"

"Nope."

"Well, I thought that was a pretty good guess. But apparently not good enough. How about, you had a kid that you never met!"

"Nope! But Nancy had one that none of us knew about!"

"Oh, come on!"

"I'm not kidding. Nancy had a baby girl, in Ohio, sometime between the time that she divorced Dick and married Bub. Her name is Maryann."

"No way!"

"Hey, I've talked to her. She sounds very nice, and she knows all about us. She was born in 1967, which I guess makes her about thirty-one."

"How'd she find us?"

"She got in touch with Terry..." (Bill's son) "...out of the blue after a detective agency helped her find out that her mother's maiden name was Nancy Weinholtz. She was born in Kent, Ohio. I can't remember Nancy spending any time in Ohio, except for when she and Dick lived in Cincinnati that year. Do you remember anything about this?"

I did. I remembered far more about it than I cared to at the time.

"Yeah, I do. Nancy moved there one fall when Lynn and Scott were really young. Mom helped with the move after Nancy got a job managing an apartment complex for a friend of hers. For the life of me, I can't remember who the friend was, but Mom said that Nancy felt bad 'living off of us', and she wanted to make a go of it on her own. Then, the next thing I knew, before the end of the school year, Nancy and the kids were back. Mom said that it did nothing but snow all the time out there, and Nancy decided that she didn't like managing an apartment complex. You don't remember any of that?"

"Nothin!"

"You're getting older."

"Yeah, right. How about the father? Do you have any idea who he is?" I had a pretty good hunch who the father had to be. Around that time, Nancy went out with a fellow named Pete, for about a year or more. He was separated from his wife, but he was Catholic and unable to get a divorce. I was around fifteen or sixteen at the time, and we used to play golf together. I had even been by Pete's apartment with Nancy on our way out to get something to eat. I really liked him. He was friendly. He had a great sense of humor. I could beat him at golf. And he bought me food. As far as I was concerned, it was a match made in heaven. I figured that, someday, Pete would be my next brother-in-law; but then, all of a sudden, it was over. When I asked Mom about it, she told me that Nancy finally decided that she couldn't wait forever for a married man. So that was that, or so I thought.

I told Bill all of this, and when we were done ruminating over the paternity issue, he sprung the next news on me.

"Well, Susan..." (by then, his new wife) "...and I invited Maryann and her husband, Sonny, to come and visit. They're flying in this weekend from Chicago."

"You, what! You don't waste any time, do you!"

"Well, she's family. She's part of Nancy and Mom; part of us. Life's too short to piddle around. I've invited them to stay with us if they feel comfortable with that, and we're having Lynn and Scott and our kids come over to meet them. Can you come down?"

It was early in the week, so I had time to make adjustments to my schedule, but Diane was ill and Phil had a championship basketball tournament which I wanted to attend. However, it soon became clear to me that I should go to Philadelphia; especially after I called Lynn (who was pregnant with her first child, Natalie) and Scott, and found them both reeling from the news, and hesitant about "getting together" so soon. Seeing the need for some mediation, I decided to call Maryann myself; and did so the next morning, only to get her answering machine. I left a rambling introductory message along with our phone number, and when I got home after work that evening, Diane told me that Maryann had called, and the two of them had a lengthy conversation. Diane said that it had been "intense, but good." She also threw in another angle that I hadn't considered.

"You know, Donn, Maryann has kids of her own, and its important for her to track down her family health history in order to have some idea what to expect."

It made good sense, and cast matters in a somewhat clearer light for me. After dinner, feeling a bit less ambivalent, I called back and found Maryann caught up in a whirlwind of emotions herself.

"This has all happened so fast. Bill and Susan have been open and generous. I really didn't expect that. But maybe we're rushing this. You see, my whole life I've wanted to know my mother. And now that I know she is dead. It's such a shock. I just have to meet the rest of you. I mean knowing that I have a sister and brother....But it's so much, so fast..."

As we talked, I was greatly relieved to find out that Maryann had been placed with a very loving family soon after she was born; and that, except for her chronic self-doubts concerning her adoption and her difficult first marriage, her life had been good. She was obviously bright, energetic and driven; traits that I assured her she shared with her biological mother and grandmother. I also told her how difficult first marriages were something else that they all had in common.

We talked on and on, including discussing the question of who her father might be. I told her I was uncomfortable revealing what I suspected, because I wasn't certain I was correct, and needed time to think things through. Maryann backed off, but it was apparent that it was only a matter of time before she would get to the bottom of it. She had too much savvy not to find out.

Eventually, we reached the issue of whether she and Sonny should stay in a motel or with Susan and Bill.

"How well do you handle smoke?"

"Smoke!"

"Yeah, Susan and Bill both smoke, and so do most of their kids. It's going to be a smokey house."

"Neither of us smoke. I can't stand smoke."

I didn't want to make too big a deal of the issue, but knowing that allergies can make some people miserable, I figured that I ought to let them know. Having gotten the cigarette matter out on the table, I pushed a little further.

"How about drinking? I don't drink very much, but my extended family likes to drink. Sometimes my family drinks a lot."

"Oh my gosh! Is it going to be safe? What's the neighborhood like? Maybe we'd better stay at a motel."

"No! No! No!, it's safe. It's perfectly safe. Susan and Bill are just like you've thought, they're wonderfully supportive and caring. And they live in a very nice neighborhood. It's a great house. Everything will be fine, I just didn't want you to be caught off guard by any of this."

After about an hour, I told Maryann that I was sure that it would become clear to her where they should stay, and that I was looking forward to meeting her and Sonny. We said goodbye. Then I called Lynn and Scott, both of whom still needed a lot of convincing that this was a good idea. It seemed to help them to know that I'd had a lengthy conversation with Maryann, and had very much enjoyed the talk. Though still cautious, they warmed to the idea of the visit.

Maryann and Sonny chose to stay with Bill and Susan, and the family gathering was a remarkable success. It probably didn't hurt that of all of Nancy's children, Maryann most closely resembled her mother. We took one look at her, and immediately the ice was broken. It was especially amazing, given their initial reticence, how Lynn and Scott took to her. Subsequently, the three of them grew close, maintaining phone contact and occasionally making visits to each other's homes.

Within a few months of our first visit, Maryann discovered that her biological father is also dead. Fortunately, although her lifelong quest to find her birth parents yielded tragic disappointments, she also discovered a cadre of caring relatives. At least this book provides a glimpse of many others she was never able to meet.

11

REFLECTIONS

As for me, nearly eleven years after Nancy's death and four years following Edie's, around the time of the publication of this book's first edition, I found myself sometimes choking up while discussing events that occurred during their illnesses. Surprisingly, it never happened while focusing on the matters described here . Then I'd be calm, in control, maybe even wryly humorous. It was at less likely times, work-related meetings or job interviews, that I unexpectedly found myself fighting back tears.

Typically, I'd be explaining something like the economic troubles that confronted us at the University of Hartford during the early nineties. I'd start off smoothly enough, with my late relatives far from mind. But their images would somehow seep into my consciousness, and suddenly I'd be trapped! Visibly upset, I'd pause to weather the emotional storm, probably leaving the impression that work demands affected me far more than they actually did. Afterwards, I'd always be embarrassed; but I'd gently forgive myself, viewing the episodes as an inevitable consequence of losing, in quick succession, several people that I dearly loved. Such episodes eventually passed, and I pretty much moved on, undoubtably aided by completing this book. But there is a paradox to writing about the deaths of loved ones. While cathartic, it is very difficult. The writing extends conscious grieving, thereby prolonging the pain; and it also raises the specter and dread of future deaths. On the other hand, the process forces recollection of wonderful memories and assists in reaching a comforting sense of resolution. In my case, I feel relief in having honored my family members; by saying what I wanted to say.

Of course, life has many ways other than writing of shepherding us towards acceptance. Continual challenges arise that prohibit allocating much thought to the past. Parenting and work demand full attention. New health crises emerge among family, friends and even ourselves. The immediacy of current circumstances push yesterday's heartbreak further and further into the past. Also, the media alert us daily to the plights of others undergoing hardships seemingly far more devastating than our own. Life forces perspective upon us.

So, I don't look back with a sense of tragic loss. Though I miss my deceased family members, I feel fortunate for having spent as much time with them as I was allowed; and I think that I have a richer appreciation for those who are still alive. I also carry with me a few deeply learned lessons about death, dying and medical care; some of which may speak to the families and close friends of severely or terminally ill individuals, and perhaps to the sick or dying patients themselves.

I learned that prognoses and timetables for extremely ill people are based on population averages and on particular physician's judgements. Thus, they may be correct or incorrect for any given person. A forecast of a few-week descent to death sometimes precedes several years of relatively stable, good health. On the other hand, an unforeseen downturn may suddenly claim one for whom recovery was expected. I've known both scenarios, and have consequently let go of clinging tightly to physicians' projections. Similarly, I no longer fixate on minor shifts in laboratory test results. Downward and upward fluctuations occur. They often reverse themselves. The emotional roller coaster ride associated with carefully monitoring these changes is exhausting. I'm no longer inclined to get too hopeful or too upset, possibly dragging others along with me, before there is a clear, reliable trend. Yet, because unexpected, precipitous declines can occur, I am more likely than before to express my love when presented an opening. I discovered the hard way that there may be no "next time."

Out of shear necessity, I also learned about assertively participating in late-stage, medical decision making. Doing so on my parents' behalf was a torturously delicate process. First, my mother and father had to request my involvement. Then, original goals had to be jettisoned as circumstances changed. Navigating these events required respecting the skills of the participating physicians, while also gauging their limitations. There was no clear, reliable map to follow. A single rule that I adopted was not to accept physicians' recommendations running counter to my parents' wishes. However, to my surprise, I discovered that under unexpected circumstances I was willing to temporarily put aside my father's clearly stated desires in the hope that longer-term benefits might be obtained from a short-term intervention. I know from experience how the most difficult decisions arise when confronting choices about initiating or withdrawing heroic, life-prolonging procedures. Sometimes a physician's rush to save someone at any cost must be resisted, but at others a measure initially considered unacceptable is warranted. I learned that, in the latter case, it is critical to obtain commitments from the physicians to withdraw life support if the desired results are not soon apparent.

Though it was difficult for me, I eventually accommodated to following a dying person's lead in discussions of impending death. I now realize that my own communication needs may be far out of touch with the dying person's. Nancy, especially, taught me the futility of trying to rush someone from denial to acceptance, especially if denial is a strategy that helped one to overcome substantial hardship earlier in life.

Unfortunately, however, denial rules out hospice care; a regrettable consequence because hospice services are truly remarkable. When a person is willing to accept impending death, hospice supports, either at home or at a facility, profoundly ease the transition for all. Finally, I learned that we all mourn in our own ways. Individual demonstrations of grief vary as much as do individual approaches to dying. Some are especially expressive; some remarkably stoic. We go about it differently. Yet, eventually, virtually all of us grieve, as long, love-filled lives inevitably involve mourning. And the loss hurts immensely. But through our grieving, we truly learn that we were blessed by love.

12

AND THEN...

With Diane's Family, Smiley Creek, Idaho, 1998

O ur immediate family was spared for nearly a decade from the next wave of deaths that confronted us. Having reached their late seventies, the age when my parents' health seriously declined, Diane's parents, Jane and

Richard Thistle, experienced major health issues of their own. Mom's was a more gradual descent brought on by chronic obstructive pulmonary disease (COPD), undoubtedly precipitated by years of smoking as a young and middle aged woman. COPD slowly diminishes lung capacity and causes susceptibility to lung infections and cardiac disease. Inability to obtain sufficient oxygen causes weakness, wheezing and steady decline until inevitable death.

Newlywed Jane and Dick Thistle, 1947

I don't recall Mom Thistle complaining as she grew weaker

and ever more dependent on supplemental oxygen. She had always been a highly energetic person, but during her last several years she didn't have the strength to confront, or worry about, all of the things that stretched her thin when she was younger. She was usually calm and appreciative for whatever assistance was provided. And Dad Thistle was always there to help her; amazingly patient, whether assisting Mom with her walker and oxygen on visits to doctors' offices, excursions to donut shops, or even trips from New Jersey to visit us in Connecticut or Diane's brother, Dick, in California or Idaho. But then, suddenly, he couldn't help any longer.

Diane, Dickie and Susan Thistle, 1955

Right up until he turned eighty, Dad was wonderfully fit. He loved to take long walks, bicycle, ski and play golf, always walking the course. However, as he grew increasingly tired and short of breath, his physicians performed sophisticated diagnostic procedures. A cardiac catheterization indicated that he had sufficient blockages to warrant bypass surgery; and Dad, anxious to squeeze as much joy and activity out of life as possible, chose to go for it.

The Thistle Family, 1954

    Mom checked into McCutcheon, a small, Quaker nursing home in their hometown of North Plainfield, NJ, while Dad went into a nearby cardiac specialty hospital for his operation. A few days before, he played 18 holes of golf with me, my brother-in-law, Dick (an emergency room physician) and our sons. Dad walked the entire course. We had a great time.

Dad and Mom Thistle, circa 1990

It was late July, 2002. Diane stayed in New Jersey, with Dick and their sister, Susan, to be with Dad during the operation. I returned to Connecticut with Dave, Phil and our daughter, Jenny, who was soon headed off for two weeks at a Quaker camp in China, Maine. We had just moved to a small, house on the campus of Watkinson School, where Diane worked as a science teacher and head of the middle school. It was my summer break from the University of Hartford, and I was busy painting rooms at our house in Windsor, CT, getting it ready to rent as a way of raising money in anticipation of soon having two sons in college. I was staying up very late painting several nights in a row, preparing the house for the early-August transfer to the tenants. Meanwhile, family friends drove Jenny to camp in Maine, where I would subsequently collect her, and several of her friends, to take us all to Wheaton College, outside of Boston, for the annual Sessions of New England Yearly Meeting of Friends (Quakers).

"Sessions" is a six-day festival/conference of business meetings, workshops, worship events and playtime held to foster social connection and spiritual nurturing, while conducting the ongoing work of New England Quakers. Diane and I have attended Sessions during most of our thirty-plus years living in Connecticut, and our kids always attended, too, because of the excellent, age-appropriate programming from pre-school through high school. For Diane to miss Sessions, in order to be with her Dad was a big, but necessary, deviation from our normal routine.

Until recently, Sessions always began on the first Saturday of August. This was just a few days after Dad's surgery. The immediate telephone report on Dad's condition from Diane was that the surgery went very well. A similarly reassuring phone call on Friday put me in a pretty good mood as I was putting the finishing touches on our house, pressuring for our renters to move in during the upcoming week. I finished painting and was ready to return to our little house on the Watkinson campus, anticipating a good night's sleep before getting up early and driving to Maine to pick up Jenny and her friends. However, a last-minute glitch caught me by surprise. On my way out of our house in Windsor, around 9:00 PM, the old, nineteen-twenties-vintage, front-door lock fell apart. I spent the next four hours scrounging around for parts and jerry-rigging a rebuild. This, kept me up far later than I had planned, and I didn't get to bed until after 2:00 AM.

Supercharged by heavy doses of caffeine, I left Connecticut about 6:00 AM on Saturday morning on the 4 ½ hour drive to China, Maine, making it there in plenty of time for the noon pickup. After I gathered the girls, we stopped for lunch at a Pizza Hut, then began the expected 3 ½ hour trek to Wheaton College in Norton, MA. Along the way, my caffeine/adrenaline rush wore off. My body was crashing. I was exhausted and really scared that I was putting the girls' safety at risk. Furthermore, the trip stretched out over a few extra hours as we hit snarling traffic jams along Interstate 95 between Portland, Maine and Boston. Consequently, I pulled in at almost every rest-stop along the way so the girls could buy snacks and go to the bathroom, while I grabbed badly needed cat naps.

Blessedly, just as dusk was approaching, we made it to Wheaton. I dropped the girls off at their dormitory and I checked myself into my dorm. Especially thankful that we had all made it to Sessions in one piece, all I wanted to do was to turn in and get a full night's sleep; but while still sitting in the car outside the dorm, I called Diane to let her know that all was well and to say goodnight. I reached her as she, Susan and Dick were heading from the hospital back to Mom and Dad's house in North Plainfield, where they'd be spending the night.

"Hey, we made it here safely, in spite of my stupid, sleep-deprived driving. Jenny and company are all settled in and I'm about ready to head up to the room and collapse for the night. How's Dad?"

"I'm so glad to hear that you made it safely. I'm sorry that I couldn't be there to help you drive, but it's really good that I'm here for Dad's sake, and to be with Sue and Dick. Dad appears to be doing great. He was up doing deep knee bends, today; and he's taking phone calls. Why don't you check in with him before calling it a night. I'm sure that he'd enjoy hearing from you."

"Sounds good. I'd like to talk to him, too. I'll call as soon as we're done."

"Thanks, he'll appreciate that. And thanks again for picking up the girls and for all that you've done this past week to get the house ready for the renters. You've got to be beat."

"Yeah, that's for sure, but the worst is behind us now. All I have to do is leave here for a few hours on Monday, drive home to meet the realtor and renters, and sign the lease. Then I can kick back and enjoy the rest of the week."

"Well, enjoy! Love you."

"Love you, too. Bye."

Diane had given me the hospital phone number, and as soon as we hung up, I called and asked for Dad's room. Really looking forward to chatting with Dad, I sat behind the wheel of our minivan, exhausted but smiling. When they put me through to his room, a nurse answered, and I quickly blurted:

"Hi, I'm Donn Weinholtz, Dick Thistle's son-in-law. Can he talk right now?"

Her response couldn't have been more shocking.

"I'm so sorry. Mr. Thistle is on the floor in the bathroom. He's just had a stroke and has fallen. We're implementing emergency procedures. I've got to go."

And she hung up.

Stunned, I thought to myself, "This is the worst. I've got to call Diane," which I immediately did.

Diane, Susan and Dick were still in the car headed along Route 22 back to North Plainfield.

"Hi, Donn. How was your talk with Dad?"

"Diane, I hate to tell you this, but Dad just had a stroke in his hospital room."

"What! Oh no, that's terrible. How bad is it? How is he?"

"I really don't know. The nurse who answered the phone said that she had to go, because they were responding to the emergency. You're going to have to get back to the hospital and find out what's happening."

Although Dad survived the stroke, the damage was severe. The left side of his body was paralyzed from the neck down. He required a feeding tube, and he was initially placed on a ventilator. The unexpected setback was devastating, but over the days, weeks, months and years that followed he doggedly persisted in his recovery efforts, never letting go of the dream that he would someday ski again.

We all knew this was delusional, but for six years we listened to Dad's hopes, including his reports of the latest research findings that he had unearthed on the internet, which he believed held the answers to fully restoring his mobility. However, rather quickly, within several weeks, Dad recovered his ability to breathe on his own, and then to swallow food. This was critical because, within months, it allowed him to join Mom at McCutcheon, the small Quaker nursing home which was not equipped for providing feeding tube care.

From the time Dad experienced his stroke until he died, he spent time in five different nursing homes. His experiences in these facilities revealed serious contrasts in quality of care, ranging from especially personal and nurturing too distant and impersonal. The differences were striking.

Once Dad's condition stabilized at the cardiac hospital, we had him moved to a modern, corporate-run nursing facility equipped to provide him with a feeding tube, as well as the physical therapy treatments necessary for him to possibly regain his ability to swallow and to strengthen his arms and legs. We naively wished that he might regain the use of the left side of his body and be able to walk again. That never happened. More realistically, we hoped Dad would soon be able to swallow, so we could have him moved to McCutcheon to be with Mom.

My primary recollection of that first stop on what became the 6-year nursing home tour was of a large, modern, attractive building seemingly designed to make a strong, favorable first impression on family members deciding on a place to provide quality long or short-term care for their loved one. The brochures by the front desk were polished products, the lobby was elegant, the rooms that we were shown were clean and well furnished, although a bit tight for two people. (Most rooms were doubles.) Also, if Dad had to stay for a very long time, and his money ran out, even with his nursing care insurance, they were qualified to accept Medicaid payments. It was fine for our immediate, short-term purposes; but as a few weeks slipped by, for several reasons, it became apparent that we didn't want it as a longer-term solution.

First, having a roommate was difficult. The man sharing the room with Dad was a nice enough person, but he had been there for a while, and his prospects for leaving were not good. He had some family in the area, including grandchildren, but they didn't visit often. He wasn't very happy. Meanwhile, Dad was having substantial difficulty communicating, and the stroke had impacted his personality. The previously very calm and considerate individual was now pretty demanding. Clearly, Dad was tremendously frustrated by his condition and impatient with the speed and degree of his recovery. Also, it seemed as though some social filters had been removed from his communications. He was likely to say things that he never would have said before, including telling occasional off-color jokes. He was still the same person, but a slightly bruised, altered version. Lying next to him, throughout the day couldn't have helped his roommate's outlook on life.

Second, it didn't take long for an institutional air of impersonality to take hold. Soon, the staff seemed to be treating Dad as just another of the many bodies housed in the facility, rather than as the special individual that we knew and loved. While the words were often appropriate, the emotion behind them simply didn't ring true. A routinized monotony emerged. This was in sharp contrast to the loving personalized care Mom was receiving at McCutcheon, just few towns away. Furthermore, Mom was staying in a room large enough to accommodate Dad, if we could just get him over there.

Third, there was something spooky about the back of the facility. Early on, while walking the halls one day, I came upon closed doors, blocking off a restricted area, which only approved personnel could enter. A staff member coming out of the wing informed me that the area beyond the doors housed the home's most difficult cases, including many people with psychiatric problems. As he passed me by, I stood by the doors listening to the disturbingly loud moaning and groaning coming from the long hallway. The haunting sounds remained the same every time that I approached the closed doors. I found myself wondering, "Will they move Dad back here, someday?"

For all of these reasons Diane, Sue, Dick (and to much lesser extent, I) decided that we'd get Dad moved as soon as he was in a position to do so. Fortunately, Dick as an emergency room physician, was in a good position to render medical advice about Dad's progress. Although he lived (and still lives) in Fresno, California, he was only a phone call away, and he could readily consult with Dad's physicians.

Although McCutcheon still could not accommodate Dad, given his need for a feeding tube, we found a spot at another, smaller, corporate-owned nursing home, just a mile or so away from Mom. It had a homier feel than the glitzy place we originally chose, and we recognized that it would be a lot easier on us all if the travel back and forth between the two nursing homes was minimized. Susan was summering in Idaho, and Dick was in Fresno, so it was up to Diane and me to get Dad settled into his new facility. We had to act fast because we also were going to be taking our son, Phil, off to his first year of college. Phil was running cross country at Dickinson College, Diane's and my alma mater, and the team had a training camp the week prior to his first-year orientation.

We managed to get both Dad and Phil situated over two days. First, we traveled from our home just outside of Hartford, Connecticut to North Plainfield, NJ, roughly three hours. That same day, with our minivan primarily loaded with Phil's clothes and college paraphernalia, we moved Dad and his modest amount of personal items in just two trips. Upon getting Dad located in his new room, we had a frank discussion with him about whether or not he wanted "heroic" measures taken in case he had a sudden physical crisis.

His response was clear. He did not want to be put on a ventilator in case he had another stroke or a heart attack. We were convinced that he was "of sound mind" and he signed an "advanced directive" indicating that this was his wish. We took a copy of the document to the nursing station.

Afterwards, we went back to Mom's and Dad's house to get a good night's sleep. Then, we headed off to Carlisle, another three-hour drive, the next morning. Of course, immediately after we breathed sighs of relief at having gotten Phil unpacked, given him goodbye hugs, and watched him go trotting off to his first practice; Diane's cell phone started ringing. It was the nursing station from Dad's floor at his new rehab center reporting that Dad had just experienced a life-threatening "episode," that he was on a ventilator, and that he was being transported to nearby Muhlenberg Hospital. We weren't quite sure what "the episode" entailed (another stroke? a heart attack? a spontaneous seizure of some sort?), but that really didn't matter. Dad had stopped breathing, his "do not resuscitate" directive had been ignored, and he was headed to a medical center where more sophisticated machines would be keeping him alive.

Shocked by the news, we immediately started the three-hour trek back to the hospital, wrestling with the unsettling thought that we would have to be making a decision about whether or not to remove Dad from life support. It was gut wrenching.

When we got to the hospital, we found Dad with a breathing tube down his throat and a feeding tube inserted in his belly, two conditions that we had all indicated that he had wanted to avoid. We subsequently found out that the nurses on the shift when Dad stopped breathing reported being unaware of the do not resuscitate directive placed in his file the night before.

Anyway, with both Susan and Dick on the other side of the country, it was up to Diane to patiently and lovingly communicate with Dad to determine if he wanted his life support measures removed. She did so, and lo and behold, he decided that he didn't want the support measures removed. He wanted to make another try at rehabbing, hoping to get back into sufficiently good shape to survive without either the ventilator or the feeding tube. It was another startling lesson regarding the need to stay attuned to your loved one's desires at any given time in potential end-of-life situations.

We will never know exactly what happened when Dad stopped breathing on his own and the breathing tube was inserted. He may have been conscious and did not object, but he may well have been unconscious and the emergency measure was simply done to him. Whatever the case, once his life was "supported" he decided not to let go. Knowing him as I did, I think that he could accept a decision to refuse heroic life support measures as a rational choice preventing a terribly diminished life requiring permanent dependence on machines. However, once having crossed that bridge to machine support, perhaps unwittingly, he likely viewed requesting removal of the tubes as suicide, a personal and religiously unacceptable option. Having been thrust into this situation, he was going to make a go of it, and not look back. And that's the way that Dad approached the rest of his life, always striving to get stronger, always looking for new challenges; until he eventually passed away from a terminal stroke, about five years later.

He soon shed the ventilator, began extensive rehab, and then managed to get off of the feeding tube, as soon as he regained his ability to swallow. Although he never regained the use of the left side of his body, he made remarkably good use of the right side. More on that, later.

Most importantly, Dad was able to move to McCutcheon Home in order to share a room with Mom. While their lives had suddenly become remarkably restricted, their time together at McCutcheon was sweet. The facility had a variety of living accommodations, from nicely appointed rooms in the main old mansion, to a row of motel-like rooms in a small separate wing, to a hallway of cozy nursing home rooms. Common meals were served in a dining room, and recreational events were often scheduled in the dining area. An especially nice feature was that there were often rooms available in the mansion, so a resident's family could visit for a night or two. We frequently took advantage of this option.

Dad's stroke occurred in early August 2002. By Christmas 2002, Dad was in McCutcheon with Mom. Then, Mom died on August 26, 2003. So, they had about 8 months together, side-by-side. Mom declined slowly and steadily. Throughout, she remained very pleasant, though noticeably weaker, month-by-month.

Dad, on the other hand, grew increasingly stronger. Although he never regained the use of the left side of his body, he made tremendous progress with what remained. Thanks to Susan's ingenuity, he learned to play a modified saxophone, single-handed. He regularly searched for paralysis cures on his computer. He put together a slideshow, which he showed and narrated for fellow residents, of his experiences in China and Southeast Asia during World War II. Then he compiled another, focused on a sailing trip he and Mom took around the Chesapeake Bay with college friends from their Rutgers' days. Following Mom's death, I accompanied Dad on three trips to Idaho so he could visit Dick and Nancy in their log home in the Sawtooth Mountains, as well as Susan in her nearby cabin. Oh, how he loved those trips!

The first time, Susan's former husband, Frank, flew to New Jersey and collected Dad, in his wheelchair. Then, they flew back to Idaho. After Dad had been there a week, I flew out, spent a day in Idaho, and flew back with Dad. We took a shuttle flight from Sun Valley to Salt Lake City and a full-size, passenger liner from Salt Lake to Newark. Over the next few years, I completed the trip two other times, each time taking Dad out to Idaho, with Dick returning him to New Jersey. We became quite familiar with the Salt Lake airport, knowing what men's restroom housed the best handicapped stall, so I could hustle Dad there just in time, before he had an accident. Helping Dad tend to his personal needs led to a level of familiarity that I never expected to have with my father-in-law; but I got used to it pretty quickly, because it enabled him some degree of freedom.

While Dad was thrilled by those trips, I found them to be pretty exhausting. Still, they were worth it, because they pleased Dad and everyone in the family so much. For me, the oddest thing about them, as with spending any lengthy amount of time with Dad following his stroke, was adjusting to the personality changes that, I earlier indicated, were becoming apparent during his first rehab assignment, and which continued for the remainder of his life. He was different than he had been prior to being stricken. Before his paralysis, Dad was as genial and thoughtful a person as you could ever meet. Afterwards, his voice somewhat strained and a little horse, he became noticeably impatient if things were not going as he hoped; and awkward in some social situations. Especially after Mom died, Dad would tell an off-color joke, now and then, and deliver pick-up lines to the nurses that he found attractive. Once paralyzed, Dad was interested in pushing himself to his limits to experience whatever he still could in the time he had left, and he fully expected all of us to help him do it. I loved him and admired him for squeezing all that he could out of life, but I'd get weary explaining to him why he wasn't going to go downhill skiing in an adapted chair, or why I couldn't drop everything and get him signed up for a new experimental brain stimulation treatment in Boston.

That's the way it was for nearly five years. Susan bore the brunt of the responsibility for visiting Dad because, except for when she was summering in Idaho, she was 30 minutes away. Diane and I made our fair share of trips down to see him; both of us making the 6-hour round trip drive once a month. We'd take him to his beloved church, go out to a local diner with old friends, and/or simply push him on wheelchair walks around McCutcheon's gardens. And I usually made an additional monthly visit to take Dad to doctors' appointments in New Jersey, or an occasional ophthalmologist check-up at the eye hospital in Philadelphia. Because my teaching schedule was confined to Tuesday-Thursday, I could always set aside a Monday or a Friday to make the trip. Diane, on the other hand, had to be at work throughout the week.

We had worked out a pretty good routine. Again, McCuthcheon was ideal for Dad's and our family's needs. The staff was incredibly supportive. We all made friends with many of the residents. The location was near all of Mom's and Dad's longtime friends, and it was very close to their church. Furthermore, McCutcheon provided family lodging at very reasonable prices during extended holiday visits. It was ideal.

But then, suddenly, we got the news. McCutcheon was closing. We had always known that this special little nursing home was teetering on the financial brink because it didn't meet the Federal standards for residents to qualify for Medicaid support. I never fully understood what those standards were, but I was aware that any nursing home dependent on all of its residents paying full freight was always in danger of going belly up. And so it was with McCutcheon; and we had to find a new home for Dad.

A frantic search resulted in another corporate-owned facility in a nearby town. It was clean, the staff seemed friendly and attentive enough. Dad could have a single, and his room was sunny. It was not McCutcheon, but we figured that it would have to do, and we would double down our efforts to make sure Dad had frequent visitors. So, we rented a U-Haul and got Dad moved. It was a crisis, but not a catastrophe. However, a catastrophe wasn't far behind.

While we were driving down to New Jersey in the midst of the preparations for the move, Diane got a cell phone call from Dick. His dear wife, Nancy, had been diagnosed with lung cancer. It was horrible news, and it just didn't seem possible. Nancy never smoked. She was a talented athlete, excelling especially at tennis. Her parents and sister were still alive and thriving. Everything about her lifestyle was healthy. How could this be happening? Was it exposure to farming chemicals in California's San Joachim Valley? There was no telling the cause, but here it was again, lung cancer, the disease that had taken my sister, Nancy.

The parallels between the two Nancy's were eerie. As I previously mentioned, Nancy Thistle's maiden name was Smith. My sister's name, before being adopted by my father, was Nancy Smith. My sister's biological father's name was Bill, as was Nancy Thistle's. Plus, Nancy Thistle's husband was Diane's brother Dick, and my sister's first husband was also Dick. And now, both had contracted lung cancer at age 50. You just couldn't make this stuff up. It was bizarrely coincidental.

The Thistle Family

For the next few years, on Diane's side of the family, we dealt with Dad's paralysis and nursing home confinement, as well as

Nancy's gradual decline while receiving her cancer treatments. The overwhelming responsibility for Nancy's care fell on Dick and the three Thistle boys, Richard (18), Bobbie (16) and Billy 12). Although Nancy maintained a wonderful spirit right until her death in the spring of 2009, the demands on the family were remarkably tough. I can't chronicle them here because it all played out 3,000 miles away, and I don't know what it all entailed. But I do know that Dick never complained, even though he maintained a full-time job as an emergency room physician, kept up two homes (one in Fresno and one in the mountains of Idaho) and oversaw the three boys. Initially, Nancy was able to contribute a lot, but as the disease wore on, Dick took on more and more responsibility. He necessarily had to run a tight ship.

On our side of the country, we made another shift in nursing homes, managing to get Dad into a wonderful, Catholic facility, the McCauley Home. McCauley is intended for retired nuns and priests, but through a remarkable set of circumstances, Dad's devoted, female computer instructor, a former novitiate, facilitated, Dad (a life-long Methodist) obtaining an open slot.

Susan continued visiting Dad most often, and did an excellent job of coordinating meeting many of Dad's needs. Diane and I went down for our regular visits, once or twice a month, and I traveled to New Jersey to pick up Dad to bring him back to Connecticut for several-day visits over the holidays. I also continued driving down a couple of times a year to take Dad to medical specialists' visits. And of course, there were the trips to Idaho, which along with providing Dad great joy, gave me an opportunity to briefly visit with Nancy, Dick and the boys.

Phil and Dad Thistle, 2008

This was our status quo until July of 2008, when Diane and I travelled to Nantucket for several days, accepting a University of Hartford colleague of mine's offer to stay at her old, Victorian house located at the heart of the island. Nantucket is beautiful, and we had a wonderful time riding our bicycles, swimming, running, and walking around the downtown, both shopping and eating in restaurants. We were taking full advantage our last, sunny morning, going for a run followed by a swim at a nearby beach. We got back to the house about 11:00 AM and were preparing for a quick lunch, allowing us to pack at a leisurely pace and catch a mid-afternoon ferry back to the mainland.

I was in the kitchen when Diane took the call, upstairs. It was another of those devastating surprise phone calls similar to others that we had received over that last two decades. Dad had just had a severe stroke at the McCauley Home, his residence for the last 18 months. He had been rushed to a nearby hospital where he was in intensive care.

Though deeply shocked by the news, we knew immediately what we had to do. There was a ferry leaving Nantucket a few hours ahead of when we had intended to leave. We hurriedly packed, and made the early ferry. After completing the 2 ¼ hour ferry ride to Hyannis, on Cape Cod, we got in our car and headed straight to New Jersey, not taking time to stop by our house in Connecticut. By the time we got to the hospital, it was almost dark. We immediately went to Dad's room. He was barely responsive. Consultations with his doctors indicated that there was nothing that could be done to improve his condition, and after lengthy talks with Susan and Dick, we decided to transfer Dad by ambulance to McCauley for hospice care.

Susan quickly arranged to fly back from Idaho, and Diane parked herself by Dad in his room at McCauley. I stayed in a room in a house on the McCauley grounds, and regularly dropped in to visit Dad and Diane. Within 24 hours of Dad's transfer back to McCauley, Susan was due to arrive at Newark airport, and I planned to pick her up and immediately bring her to McCauley.

Unfortunately, Susan's planes were delayed a few hours, but this inconvenience didn't seem too problematic because it was a straight shot of about 20 minutes on Interstate 78, from the airport back to MacCauley. But as we hustled to return, when we were only a few minutes away, Diane called, tearfully telling us that Dad had just died. It was heartbreaking. Dad and Susan had been so close, and she had done everything she could to get there to be with him at the end. Yet, we just missed, literally by a few short minutes. After we entered the room and Diane and Susan hugged, Diane and I left, so Susan could have time alone with Dad.

For me, the time immediately after Dad's death is a complete blur. I don't remember anything until his memorial service, when things come back into focus. Like Mom, Dad had a lovely service at Wilson Memorial Union Church in Watchung, New Jersey, where Mom and Dad had been devoted attenders throughout their retirement years. The service was presided over by Reverend Barbara Peters, who had been a great source of strength and comfort for Dad and our family throughout the trials of Mom's and Dad's combined illnesses, Mom's death, Dad's grieving and then Dad's death. Diane, Susan, Dick and I all spoke at the service. They all offered lovely, moving messages honoring their beloved Father. I was the last to speak.

The Thistles, Juilianos and Weinholtz's at Dad Thistle's Memorial Service - 2008

Throughout my adult life, I've done a lot of extemporaneous public speaking, and I have presided at many Quaker memorial services. So, I felt no hesitation about offering a heartfelt message at Dad's service. I looked forward to it. I had a clear message in my head, and I started strongly; but before long, I found myself choking up and struggling to get through. I regained my footing and finished off ok, but I was baffled at the deep emotion that seemingly came up out of nowhere.

Later, I recalled that following his initial stroke, as I have previously mentioned, Dad was transformed. He was partially paralyzed, constantly challenged and emotionally different from the man we had all known and loved. Furthermore, the immediate and ongoing demands of his care were so pressing that we never had the opportunity to mourn the version of Dad that we lost. We (or at least I) just pushed ahead, while suppressing the hurt of the loss. After all, how do you grieve the departure of one who is still among you?

My message at the service involved honoring both the remarkably kind and supportive Dad we knew before the stroke and the more difficult Dad who persevered so heroically for over five years afterwards. I really wanted to alert the nursing home staff who were attending the service about the wonderful man they had missed meeting. In juxtaposing Dad before and after his stroke, it suddenly hit me just how much I missed pre-stroke Dad. He had been long gone, and I had never shed a tear. Meanwhile, I had grown closer to Dad during his post-stroke years. The many trips down to New Jersey to take him to the doctors, the nursing home moves, the trips to Idaho, changing his soiled clothes, washing him, talking about impending death, listening to him explain how he planned to go skiing again; all of these things endeared him that much more to me. (Even though I couldn't tell if he felt any closer to me. Post-stroke Dad didn't exude affection.)

Anyway, suddenly in the middle of my message, I was caught in a tangle of grief for the Dad I originally knew and the very different Dad that I helped care for over the last five-plus years. At least, that's what I think happened. I can't really be sure, but it makes good sense to me. And oh yeah, there was one other thing that probably contributed to me being emotionally labile. The service was held on August 13, 2008, my own Mom's birthday. She would have been 94.

Despite her cancer treatments, Nancy Thistle had been strong enough to fly, with Dick and the boys, from California to New Jersey for Dad's memorial service. Their family and our family, including Dave's girlfriend at the time, Christina, and Jenny's boyfriend and future husband, Matt, all stayed at a motel not too far away from Mom and Dad's church. It had a large, indoor swimming pool and the evening after the service we all hung out at the pool. Nancy was in good spirits and was well enough to fully participate in the fun in and out of the water. I remember her spending time aside with Phil, who was particularly grieving Dad's passing. He later shared with me how comforting talking to Nancy had been. Diane and I were thankful for Nancy's presence, as well as for all that Dick, Richard, Bobby and Billy had done to support her since she had fallen ill. It was a special moment filled with a great sense of loss, but also love and appreciation for each other. It was also the last time that we would all spend time with Nancy. Eight months later, on April 22, 2009, Nancy died. She was 52.

Richard and Nancy Thistle

About a month before Nancy's death, Diane took some time during her March spring break to visit Nancy and Dick. Susan followed the week after. Both helped out around the house and spent precious time visiting with the entire family. And both later commented on how "present" Nancy was, despite having grown so much weaker since the previous August. Neither assumed that Nancy would pass so soon after they left. When Dick called with the sad news, it was yet another shock. Such calls are always a shock. The finality always hurts, so badly.

Diane quickly made plans to fly to Fresno to help Dick arrange Nancy's funeral. I began looking into flight arrangements for Dave (who was living in Brooklyn, NY), Phil, Jenny and me to fly out a few days later in time to attend the service. Both Phil and Jenny were attending the University of Hartford; so they were nearby. We planned to drive to New York, pick up Dave, then catch a flight out of Newark. All was unfolding smoothly. Then the day before we were to leave, our 14-year-old dog, Smiley, died a sudden and painful death brought on by a case of bloat (a severe twisting of the stomach) which proved untreatable in spite of her getting immediate care. Jenny, Phil and I were with Smiley when our veterinarian put her to sleep. She was such a good dog, and as I held her, I remember thinking, "Do we have to be going through this right now!"

After Smiley was laid down, I called Diane to tell her the bad news. She was in the midst of everyone grieving the loss of Nancy and making funeral arrangements; so she was in no position to take it too hard. But as fate would have it, when she flew home from Fresno, a few days later than the rest of us, the airplane movie was, *"Marley and Me,"* a Tom Hanks comedy about a beloved dog, with a tear-jerking ending. It hit Diane hard.

Following the traumatic interruption of Smiley's death, the next day we managed to make it to Brooklyn, pick up Dave, get to Newark Airport and catch our flight to Fresno. We all stayed with Dick and the boys, as did Susan. Nancy's service, held at New Hope Community Church on April 25th, 2009, was a lovely tribute to a beautiful spirit.

Blessedly, within a few years Dick met Lisa, a Fresno State University faculty member with three children of her own. Lisa is smart, friendly, and athletic; and she loves the mountains of Idaho. She and Dick have been happy life partners ever since.

Bill and Susan

Three years later on April 7, 2012, my brother Bill's wife of 14 years, Susan, died due to a rapidly spreading cancer. I was stunned when I received the news, Sue, who was only 60 at the time of her death had survived a brain aneurism prior to meeting Bill, and had been an ardent advocate for aneurysm and brain-bleed survivors for as long as we had known her. I had always assumed that Sue would be susceptible to a debilitating stroke, but I'd chosen not to think much about it. Now, I got a phone call from Bill's son, Terry, telling me Sue had just died, and I hadn't even known that she was sick.

Sue had always been warm and gracious to Diane, me and our adult children; hosting us during Christmas holiday visits, remembering birthdays etc. But we were never as close as we had been with Edie, with whom we had gone through so many formative experiences over so many years. Rather than feeling a deep personal setback, I was more worried about Bill. How would he hold up under another terrible loss?

Sitting at Bill's table at the luncheon reception following Sue's funeral, my concerns were allayed. Bill was visibly shaken; but as he explained what a good wife and friend Sue had been, while downing a few Manhattans, I could tell that, resilient as always, he would press on. Then, six months later, he married Barbara!

Bill and Barbara had gone to high school together and had been friends, but they had never dated. They only reconnected because Barbara and Sue were friends through an arts and crafts organization to which they both belonged. When Sue became ill, Barbara provided her, and Bill, with a lot of support. After Sue's death, one thing led to another. At 74 years old, and not wishing to waste any time, Barbara and Bill got engaged and married. She for the second time, and Bill for the fourth.

Barbara, Bill and Lynn

The wedding occurred on October 27th, 2012, Diane's birthday, and just a few days after Superstorm Sandy ripped through the Middle Atlantic states. Gas was in short supply, and we weren't sure that we could fill up on our way down from

Connecticut, or on our way back. It was touch and go, but we made it. The wedding and reception were joyous occasions, attended by a lot of people from both the bride and groom's family and friends. I was taken aback by the fact that my brother was marrying for the 4th time, but he seemed so pleased that I figured, "Oh, so what! Just go with it."

The more that we got to know Barbara, the more we appreciated what a warm, thoughtful, creative person she was. We really hit it off great, and we were very happy for her and Bill. Then, after 2 ½ years of marriage, Barbara, another smoker, died of lung cancer. Rocked by the tragedy, Bill swore off marriage; but it wasn't too long before he was dating Betty, a steady companion who he has been seeing ever since 2015. Diane and I have only seen Betty a few times, but she and Bill seem to have a supportive arrangement, which has included occasional trips to Florida to visit Betty's children.

I rarely get to Philadelphia anymore, so my visits with Bill are pretty much limited to phone calls that I initiate, and texts, which are just as likely to come from Bill, telling me to wish Diane or any of our kids a " Happy Birthday." I called just the other day, and caught Bill, with his dog Bella, driving back home from Delaware, where he was able to get discounted, low-tax cigarettes and liquor. Bill was gleeful over saving nearly $100 on his purchases, while only having to drive 2 ½ hours, round trip. Having long-ago given up on trying to get Bill to quit, or even moderate somewhat, his smoking and drinking habits; I just laughed at my crusty, 83 year-old brother, who insisted on living his life "his way."

"They must be thrilled to see you come walking through the door."

"You betcha, Brother."

Diane and I have been blessed with 51 years of marriage, a wonderful family, satisfying jobs, great friends, and overall good health. We have so many reasons to be grateful. But of course, death is relentless. Like everyone else in the world, we will continue to deal with difficult losses, including our own deaths. Over the last several years some good friends have passed away. As best we could, we've tried to support their families through their grief and transitions. Based on those experiences, I take comfort in the fact that if something happens to me, first, Diane will be surrounded by our kids, grandkids, extended family, and a remarkable group of women, and some men, who will provide loving support. On the other hand, if Diane dies first, who knows how I'll hold up. I'm not going to spend further time here speculating about what lies ahead. Some possibilities are just too painful to think about, and it's all so unpredictable, anyway. It hardly seems worth it.

But there is, for sure, one thing about which I'm absolutely certain. When my time comes, just like my Mom, "I'd rather go out smiling."

The Combined Thistle, Juiliano and Weinholtz Families at Bobby and Betsy Thistle's Wedding - Stanley Idaho, 2023

ABOUT THE AUTHOR

1 Year-Old Donn in Ocean City

Donn Weinholtz grew up in suburban Philadelphia, having the good fortune to spend his summers in Ocean City, New Jersey. Although not much of a ball player himself, he is a life-long, die-hard Phillies fan.

Donn is also an emeritus Professor at the University of Hartford (CT). Over 29 years, he served the University in various capacities; directing the Doctoral Program in Educational Leadership, serving as dean of the University's College of Education, Nursing and Health Professions, chairing the Faculty Senate and sitting on the University's Board of Regents. He also taught graduate courses in professional ethics, statistics and research methods, as well as undergraduate courses in Leadership and American Studies.

He is a Quaker, active among Friends in Hartford, New England and the U.S.; and has served as clerk of Hartford Monthly Meeting and on New England Yearly Meeting's Permanent Board. He was the founding editor of Friends Association for Higher Education's online publication, *Quaker Higher Education*, and has twice served as FAHE's clerk. He has also served as one of New England Yearly Meeting's representatives to Friends Committee for National Legislation.

With his wife, Diane, a recently retired, science teacher and school principal, Donn has co-facilitated many Help Increase the Peace Program (HIPP) trainings, including working with approximately 2,000 teachers in Rwanda, Africa.

Diane and Donn are the parents of three grown children and grandparents of four ranging from 9-2.

Made in the USA
Coppell, TX
15 June 2024